Raw Feet

DC Teen Voices
Presented by Writopia Lab,
DC Regional Affiliate for The Scholastic Writing Awards

Written and Published by
Select Authors of the 2013 DC Scholastic Writing Awards
Administered by Writopia Lab
www.writopialab.org

Dedicated to all who inspire us....

Chimamanda Ngozi Adichie, Junot Diaz, Gabriel Garcia Marquez, Neil Gaiman, Douglas Adams, Markus Zusak, Tamora Pierce, John Green, Jean-Dominique Bauby, J.R.R. Tolkien, J.K. Rowling, Lev Grossman, Robert Pirsig, that lady on the metro who read me psalms, Lily Evans Potter, Suzanne Collins, Jhumpa Lahiri, Princess Diana, Stephen Chbosky, Robert Frost, Jill Scott, Ariel Adams, Janie Starks, Mel Bochner, Ed Sheeran, Jane Austen, Tina Fey, Augustus Waters, Isaac Asimov, Steve Alten, Jehane Noujaim, Music, Food, and Charles Dickens.

contents

foreword

I grew up wanting to be a writer. From about the time I could hold a pencil, I wrote. I wrote lists of my favorite colors, plays that my sister and I would put on, songs that I paraded around the house singing. I wrote letters to imaginary pen pals. I wrote stories about my stuffed animals. Any time my parents had the audacity to think I'd done something wrong—you better believe I wrote my side of that story!

Writing was a way to revisit important moments, to make sense of the world, to make up alternate versions, to connect with other people, to feel understood. As I grew up, I would walk down the street and think about how everyone had their own story, and be amazed by the stories in the world. I'd rush home to get the words down. When I hit college, I majored in English with a "concentration" in creative writing.

But, as graduation loomed closer, I decided to apply to law school.

At the time, I came up with what seemed like a good enough reason: I'd been going to school for basically my entire life, and I was pretty good at it. I wasn't ready to stop being a student, and I didn't specifically *not* want to go to law school.

Truthfully, I was waiting for someone to tell me to be a writer instead. But no one did. My parents would have supported any decision I made, but they weren't writers. My close friends weren't writers, either; in fact, many of them were applying to law school, too. That was the safe option, the one that saved me from having to face a deep fear—that I could try my hand at writing professionally, and fail miserably.

As you may imagine, law school led to the bar exam, which led to a job at a law firm, where I worked long hours and wore suits—except on weekends, when we were allowed to wear jeans. One particular Saturday, because no one else was there and because I felt like it, I cartwheeled down the hall, past the partners' offices. There wasn't much time left over for creative writing. It was the first time in my life that I wasn't actively working on some piece of fiction or memoir. But I reminded myself that I was growing up, I had a new career, and I felt okay about it.

And then, suddenly, it wasn't okay anymore.

I began to take a little time for myself every day or so, just five or ten minutes, to sit and stare off into space and make up stories. I always closed my office door, so no one would see me zoning out like that. Sometimes the stories would be inspired by things that happened in the office; like one day, a potential client came in and confessed to embezzling funds from her job. She was terrified of being sent away and having to leave her kids. I too wondered what would happen to them. Would their stepfather stick around or leave? Would they be able to forgive their mom? I made up other stories, too—a bunch of them involved my leaving law firm life for the life of a writer. I thought if I ever started writing again, maybe I'd start with a novel for kids, because it would be shorter.

Around this time, I turned to the Internet and found a community of people who wrote for kids and teens. They all seemed to know each other, posting pictures from conferences, commenting on each other's blogs. Like a college student pledging a sorority, I desperately wanted to be in their crowd. The idea of never having the opportunity to join them was scarier than the idea of trying and being turned down. I knew my only shot was to write my way in, and so I started writing.

I never stopped. Now I write all day, every day. Except on Tuesdays, when I go to my *other* job. I teach a writing workshop at Writopia Lab.

Officially, Writopia is a not-for-profit organization that seeks to foster joy, literacy, and critical thinking in all young people through creative writing.

To me, Writopia is a place of possibility. It's a safe haven where kids can zone out with no shame, where they can cartwheel for the sake of getting the details exactly right, where they can write whatever comes to mind—realistic fiction, fantasy, memoir, silly stories, brilliant stories, stories that may anger their parents, or scare them. It's a place where their work is taken seriously, where they are encouraged to submit to places like the Scholastic Art & Writing Awards, and they do—because at a very young age they know something I didn't come to terms with until much later: You can't succeed at anything, even the thing you love best, unless you're willing to risk failure.

As the writers whom you'll meet on the following pages no doubt know, success tastes so much the sweeter for it.

I don't regret the path I took to the job I have now, but when I talk to my students, I tell them that I don't think anyone should go to law school unless they actually want to be a lawyer. I tell them not to let uncertainty deter them from doing the thing they want most to do. I tell them that the writer's life, if not necessarily a safe option for the future, is always a legitimate one. And I tell them something else I've learned—that writing is less a solitary experience, and more about community. These kids share their work, they take in the compliments and critiques, they keep going, they make it better.

I like to think I'm a good teacher, but the truth is, I get back much more than I give. When I look at my Tuesday group, eight students and one teacher, I think we add up to much more than the sum of the parts.

These days, most days, I work longer hours than I ever did at the law firm—though I never have to put on a suit!—and whether I'm having a good writing day or a bad one, I know it's worth the risk, and I know I'm not in it on my own. That's what I wish someone had told me before I started law school, and what I tell every kid who comes to me saying she wants to be a writer when she grows up.

Courtney Sheinmel
Author of All the Things You Are, Sincerely, Positively, *and* My So-Called Family

www.courtneysheinmel.com

introduction

We've always thought of writing as a way to learn someone, learn the curves of their personality and the wounds of their heart, without actually getting to know them in the first place. The teen writers who have shared their works in this book have given you the opportunity to learn them. They have given you their poetry, their short stories, personal memoirs. They have given you their words.

We have all felt our own sensations of "raw feet," whether sore and worn from work and walking, scraped and blistered by adversity, or pink and vulnerable in their newness. Our feet are raw because we have not yet grown the shields that come from the years of harsh weather that one must be accustomed to in our world. Our feet are raw because we still possess the innocence of youth. Our feet are raw because we have lost that innocence, because we've outgrown that smooth unbroken skin, because we have learned the burdens that all of us must carry. We are in between the soft world of children and the sharper, harder world of adults.

Turn the page. Listen to our stories, the words that we choose to define who we are. With the hopes that we can show you a window into a new perspective— an understanding of what it means to stand not just in our shoes, but in our feet—we give you the collected works of *DC Teen Voices*.

The Editorial Team

"There is nothing to writing.
All you do is sit down at a typewriter and bleed."
-- Ernest Hemingway

sixteen ain't grown

by any means necessary.
i've always loved a man who wasn't
afraid of getting his hands dirty.
my father.

my baby brother is having a baby, and with him only
being sixteen, there is no room for the questions of
"are you ready?" because in this situation, he has no
choice. no options of, "i wish i would have waited,"
because he didn't. our parents will demand the answers
to the questions of "how will you provide for your
child?" and "what about your education?" but i knew
he would figure it all out. i asked him how would he
teach his daughter about god. he said, *"i'll take her to
church"* as if it were a simple task, and in this response, i
realized why i've stopped believing.

*"when we were little, i used to think daddy was god, you know.
in my eyes, his sins weren't really sins, just clean mistakes."*

baby brother's cold stare showed me he didn't
understand, and honestly, i didn't know why i would
expect otherwise. my father was good to us, but he
wasn't necessarily a good man. he did whatever was
necessary to put food on the table even if it meant
holding up the last supper. and afterwards, would bow
down and ask for forgiveness. and maybe that's why i
always thought that loving someone was to hurt them
and then make them feel better because, in my
household, god forgave easily.

"your baby girl will see you as god, your words holding more meaning than the red scriptures of the holy book. she will worship you, baby brother. she will try to mirror what she sees, just to make you smile. a proud father makes a blessed daughter and we all pray for blessings, don't we? it was daddy who told me jesus did not die for our sins but that he was pinned to the cross for his own. and as a man of god, i ask you, how will you teach your daughter about him?"

i am going to be a father. 16 ain't grown but i've been a man for a minute. a father. holding her beliefs in my rough hands until she is old enough to realize that i too am just human, a baby girl of my own, i'm nothing but a baby. and truthfully, you're never really ready for fatherhood. saying it over and over still does not make it register that pampers and pacifiers will be coming out of my pocket. and if i lie enough, i'll eventually believe that it isn't true. what does it mean to love someone like your own when your own disowns you? a teenage father doesn't align with doctors and lawyers. what does it mean to be a man? my father was only a provider. a distorted image in god's likeness. when he turned water into wine to intoxicate the minds of his following. so what stories will i tell my child about my childhood?

Asia Alston, Grade 11
Duke Ellington School of the Arts
Washington, DC
Poetry, Honorable Mention

memoir
(excerpted)

"*Ektashundor* artwork *banaoamarjunno!*" my mother would say.

When I was five years old, I would giggle so hard after hearing these words that I would simply fall onto the floor and bring my mother's giggles with me. Why this sentence made me giggle, I'm not so sure, because the only word I comprehended was the English part— "ah–wook"—and everything else sounded like sharp syllables of mush. A goofy-noise-ritual seemed plausible, missioned to make me laugh. Yet, throughout my childhood, I realized that this would become the phrase that commenced the plainly-worded 'art time'— a time that my imagination was a careless paint bomb, ready to explode...even on my mother.

We were fond of the beautiful messes we created. We tilted our heads the same way when we evaluated. Like her, I was craving to let my mind wander—to express the way time passed, whether it was sublime, a wish, or even an undeveloped thought. It had to be in front of me—converted from my mind, through the air, like some sort of magic. I wanted her to see my dreams, exactly as I dreamt them, during the hours of night and day—when I slept, when I lost insight. I wanted to show her exactly what I saw—the godly tigers that asked me to follow without explanation, when I jumped into the book, became the same size as Dr. Doolittle, and saved the animals of the circus. Or the time that Tarzan swept me off my feet, or the morning I found myself napping upon the warm belly of Baloo the bear.

My mind became a clock, instinctively chiming when it was time to prepare the spare room, and excitement consumed me. It was a time that my mother and I valued, shared what we imagined and dreamed: I, as silly as I was, to someday transform into a cat...while my mother's dream was selfless. It was to ensure that the future, and all my dreams, whatever they would be, came true, as our artistic energies would flow beyond that room, and I would one day unleash it, for the world.

Not all of my mother's stories were compelling to the young, wild, and naïve girl that I was. But, of course, there was always one story that enthused the geeky and passionate little girl in me: when she lived in Bengal, and among a generation of wild cats. That is, until she realized she would have to take them back to their natural home, a jungle near Rajshahi—the very place a young Rudyard Kipling found inspiration to set his classic *Jungle Book*—a story that, coincidentally, greeted me again like fate, and made me giggle again when I thought of the kindred and silly Baloo. I look back now at my childhood, and this story was one of many that sparked my passion for the world of animals.

My mother would remind me after this story that she saw her father's ambitiousness and his nature-spirited mother in me, "a humble little Jane," she would smile and say. This 'Jane' she referred to, whether it was Tarzan's bride I was strangely jealous of, was actually the humble woman who "revolutionized mankind"— Jane Goodall, and not surprisingly, one of the most inspirational people who inspires me today. I was privileged enough to meet her, and have come to love her moving desire for hope: for humanity and animals and their world—one in which we live in harmony with nature. That we, as human beings, have a duty to love, embrace, and reciprocate care for a world that shelters us. Jane Goodall's legacy and groundbreaking work—understanding evolution, behavior, and the patterns of nature, helping us come closer to understanding ourselves—how we can preserve that very life in the future—is the reason why doing the same has become a part of my dreams.

The many afternoons of 'art time' I have my mother to thank for, because I never imagined then how the simple word 'artwork' would caress me as I would grow. Through art, I have been able to expand my imagination to pick out the unapparent structures and patterns in my everyday world. It has become my way of life, and, like a sculptor, helps me to carve what I am truly capable of seeing. I have learned that it even helps us to preserve, even personality, from the loved ones I spend time with who have Alzheimer's. It has created so many precious memories for me, like when Lucy, the silly Orangutan I volunteered with at the D.C. Zoo, immediately recognized a picture I drew of her, and showed me all of her teeth...what was actually an awkward *smile*. I realize that my mother has indirectly, and miraculously, brought art into my life purposefully, and not just as a simple childhood pastime. It is almost philosophical, it unravels itself beautifully in everything we see, and has helped me especially to notice the little things in nature that are simply left unnoticed.

Although I continue to be an artist and cultural dancer like my mother, I still keep my grandfather's ambition and his mother's 'natural' spirit inside me. Through all these connections of my different passions, I hope not only to be "wildlife jungle girl," but, like Jane Goodall, a carrier of jungle peace. Everywhere I will go, I hope to not only learn more about people and embrace life through all of its artistic aesthetics, but as a keen observer of natural life, I hope to become a future leader of hope and a humble analyzer of mankind. As Gandhi wishes, I intend to be the change I wish to see in the world.

Lauren Andalib, Grade 12
Fairfax High School
Fairfax, VA
Personal Essay, Honorable Mention

the staircase

I caught myself, yesterday,
Just staring at the sky

I was inside, then
I had climbed the stairs in the morning.
Walking down the steps, on the top floor
I saw my kingdom outside the windowed stairwell.
The wind was blowing, and trees were dancing,
Luminescent foliage,
And tile roofs in the background,
Subtle shades of gray.
I didn't look for very long,
I had another class to get to.

I walked down a flight of stairs
And then I saw that my kingdom had gone
The two-story windows showed only the sky now,
The memory of clouds, white wisps flying past
The bell rang
I was late

I rushed down another flight.
At ground level, as I was rushing back into the hallway,
I glimpsed the door that lead outside
And
I stopped
All my view was, was a street
A parked car
And litter
A leaf blew across my landscape
Flitting away

I turned and left,
For after all,
I had to climb the staircase
to get to fourth period.

Elena Asofsky, Grade 8
Lakelands Park Middle School
Gaithersburg, MD
Poetry, Silver Key

dried blood
(excerpted)

"... Stay inside, avoid contact with suspicious persons, and lock your doors. People that have contracted the disease are violent..."

It stares blankly at the screen for a moment, unsure if it is food or not. A noise echoes down to it from the east. Noise means living meat. Food. It begins to shamble off to the east, trying to fulfill the most basic of instincts, hunger. The road is a maze of abandoned cars, some smeared with blood. A few have dead meat.

Others walk with it, staring blankly at the horizon with jaws agape. Separate, but together in their desire to feed. Some have wounds in their bodies, the bleeding long since stopped. Dried blood does not leak from open holes. It barely sees the others, its mind consumed by the promise of food.

Passing by one of the cars, it notices a brown furred thing sitting idly on a seat. It meets the thing's cold, black stare...

"Come on daddy!" the little girl exclaims, eyes wide. Lights, sounds, and smells surround it as they move through bright stands, lighting up the night sky like neon fire.

A voice, familiar yet forgotten, responds, "Fine, Sally, let's go get you a prize!"

The girl squeals happily.

It moves at the tugging of this small one, towards a stand with a bigger man inside. It hands the other man green paper, and is given a stack of balls. Picking one up, it throws it at a tower of bottles, and watches as they collapse. The man gives him a brown furred thing, a small bear, as reward. It gives the bear to the girl, who hugs it tightly. It is content, but it can't remember why.

It blinks its eyes, and then moves east once more. The sounds continue to draw it on, tempting it with the knowledge of food. Moving through the cluttered streets and silent roads, it vaguely realizes that the others have left it behind.

Eventually, the cars clear and the tall buildings disappear. There's movement to the left, its gaze snaps towards a broken window. Inside, bright things sparkle in the flickering light, little rings and chains with stones. It moves closer to find a collection of trinkets on deep red cloth. One piece catches its eye, a small gold circle with a cut stone on top.

It's on its knees, staring up at a woman. In its hands is a small box, the light from a lamp glinting off the stone within. The woman looks amazed, scared. Then happy, nodding, she says something but the tears muffle her voice. It stands, old feelings moving through its blood. Not hunger, not adrenaline, something gentle, warm. It wraps its arms around her, but not in attack. It strokes her back as she embraces it.

This was a beginning, a new start, and it was excited yet terrified. In the woman's arms, though, it would not fear or falter. It held her tightly, all the world but them fading away as they embraced underneath a moonless sky.

It's further down the road now, beyond the town. Staring blankly ahead as it moves in the direction of food. Those noises continue, a siren call to its primal needs. But something else lingers, that alien warmth in its dried blood. The road is narrow now, the buildings replaced by wood and green leaves.

The forest to its left clears for a few feet, showing it a clearing in the dense trees. Tall grey stone pillars spot the grass. Flowers are placed next to some. It stops in front of a black, sealed iron gate, a dull sting growing in its chest. Its eyes sting too, as its mind turns, but nothing comes of it. It cannot shed tears anymore.

It is crying, kneeling over the woman once again, something above him beeping loudly. But she is lying in bed, pale, the smell of death hanging softly in the air. Her life is nearly over. But she smiles, comforts it, takes its hand in hers. It holds onto her, the warmth from her hand drifting away. Crying, begging, pleading to whatever will listen to its thoughts.

A smaller voice asks for its mother. It's the girl who received the brown furred thing. She looks fragile, scared. The woman takes her hand, too.

"Don't worry about me, I'm going away now, I might be gone for awhile... but I'll see you again, someday," the woman says, to the girl, to it. Smiling for them despite her halting breath, her failing heart.

The beeping stops for a moment, before one loud beep drones on. It looks up, to the sad, scared, and confused girl. It found a reason to keep going in her soft brown eyes, but it can't remember that reason now. There is pain, other visions flirt with its mind, of the woman and it together. Tempting it to surrender, lay down and escape the pain. But the girl needs it. It would suffer through any pain for that girl.

Looking down at the woman's still face, he says, "Someday... but not today." Quiet enough that the girl can't hear, silent enough that maybe the woman might.

It continues walking, past the stone-covered field. Instinct barely covering the turmoil inside it, old feelings and forgotten pain reawakened. The noise continues to call it east, to food.

Hours, maybe days later it finds a new town. Lights are still on in this one, the noises come from there. It walks on, passing by dead and rotten meat. One of the bodies wears a dress, torn flower patterns covering its small frame. The meat reminds it of the girl, who had meant so much in a life gone by.

They're inside a house. Something is hitting the door, moaning and scratching. He stands over the girl, reassuring her. He tells her to run, escape from this hell.

She asks, "Will I see you again?"

He nods, smiling for her, to hold the tears back.

Her eyes see the lie, like they had when her mother died, but she nods and escapes the house. He lets the tears run as he watches his girl sprint outside. The door breaks, but he doesn't acknowledge it. He just falls to his knees, watching his girl run.

Somewhere, he knows that letting the monsters get him is a fate worse than death. Somewhere, he knows that letting the monsters get him will give Sally more time.

The girl is all that matters now. He would go through any pain for her.

It has found the noise at last, but its steps are slower now. The hunger is replaced by pain beyond its flesh, sparking through its dried blood. It sees living meat, with lights and tools of death. The noise comes from behind them and the barricade. The bodies of others, like it, litter the street.

Somewhere, it knows that it will die here. Just as it knew its death in an old life. Just as it knows that it can't see the girl, Sally, his girl, ever again.

The marines gun down the zombie, which had fallen for the same trap as the other dozens, dead on the street. One of the foremost men looks at the most recent kill curiously.

"What's wrong Frank, don't tell me you're going soft?" laughs a man to his left.

"It's nothing," Frank replies, "Just thought I heard it say something. Sounded like 'ally'..."

It lay on the ground, one more body in a world of corpses. Its dried blood ran freely, watered by unwept tears. The pain of a past life leaked away, and the torment of its new prison turned to dust as it died.

Ian Austin, Grade 11
Damascus High School
Damascus, MD
Science Fiction / Fantasy, Silver Key

in the land of opportunity

In the land of opportunity
I'm at a standstill like scarecrows
I remember back in the day
When I had to share clothes
Too many nights with no lights
And the bed cold with no heat
So we had to sit near a stove
Damn...
I still remember them days
Moms had a lil' job
But it was minimum wage
As a young'un I was street smart
But not as good at the grades
Why you think it's called "the trap"?
'Cause the hood is a MAZE!
I was pushin' quarter pounds of dat pack
Try'na prosper in poverty
A part of me purposely perpin'
So please pardon me
Police be try'na bother me
People tend to push me
I wasn't thinking logically
That's when dem' people took me
Now, I'm trapped in a cage
In the land of opportunity
And it's kind of sad
'Cause things are better in here
Than out where I used to be

No way out
My opportunities are bare
Hoping that when I'm free
The land will still be there

AZ, Grade 11
Free Minds Book Club and Writing Workshop
Washington, DC
Poetry, Silver Key

american zodiac

The Ram
You see it in the paths two cars take before a collision,
in the bumping inflections of speeches unspoken,
as if you could take your stroboscope and clap down
that fleeting pulse of life that turns the sand between
children's toes into the glass
cutting lies in the gray face of morning.

The Bull
You see it in the skeleton houses nestled in each
wrinkle of the mountain,
good dreams the sandman sprinkled upon sleeping eyes
that have long since opened.
Whose beams ache to be raised from ribcage to sky in
an open-armed archway
for limping children to pass under
but now only form the highway-side crosses of
cancelled-out maybe-somedays.

The Twins
You see it in the grasp of the blind couple on the other
side of the tracks,
glimpsed only through passing metro cars,
whose glazed eyes cannot see the flashing lights at the
edges of life
that warn of the incoming day.
Who know true joy is not as flat as *attention: doors opening*
and loss is not as simple as *caution: doors closing.*

The Crab

You see it in the cornerpeople who thrust papers at
you, pleading for your pocket,
there's-children-in-Africa, problems-here-at-home, be-
the-change-you-wish-to-see,
who will keep throwing good intentions into the stars
until fliers rain down like manna from the sky.

The Lion

You see it in the laughter-lipped veteran who floats
through the Capitol,
occasionally joining sticky-handed school groups or
camera-necklaced couples,
always making that same joke about Taney
fixing the courtroom clock five minutes early,
always waiting for his audience to laugh
and thinking, *tomorrow, tomorrow.*

The Maiden

You see it in the decades sprinkled across the face of
the woman who rides the school bus,
watching each little now get on with muddied sneaker
and slipping hair tie,
thinking of the glorious before,
when the world was flat and the streets were narrow,
and when there was no fear of the after etched into her
leather-beaten skin.

The Scales

You see it in the statue of the woman wading in the
silver lake
that you found stumbling blindfolded through acres of
forest. The two open hands,
palms up, hold copper coins of open-mouthed muses
who tell you to turn around and forget the shiver of

stone shoulders.
It is nothing, they say, *but the sound of cloth peeled from the eyes.*

The Scorpion
You see it in the *er* the billboards throw at the person
sitting next to you,
faster, cleaner, slimmer, primmer,
preached from magazines as if they were mountains,
the new Decalogue of *thou shalt nots*
screamed by the people who eat their own throats
and choke out broken words to
silent ceiling fan psychiatrists
in the nakedness of their own minds.

The Archer
You see it in the open hands of the girl in the
abandoned amphitheater
who is more light than flesh, carving the spring-
speckled air with her arms,
a one-ended embrace with no purpose
but to touch the salt of stars.

The Sea-Goat
You see it in the flatness of empty parking lots of rust-
and-dust towns
whose horizon summits and trenches were carved
from,
sprawling and sprawling and sprawling,
only good for endless rides of anger or ecstasy
by the middle children of society
who look for no cornucopia of meaning in the asphalt
of memory.

The Water-Bearer
You see it in the cupped hands of your niece who
whispers hot gusts of secrets into your ear
that tell of forgotten yesterdays and mindless
tomorrows
and a truckload of brimming before-I-die's you
promised, you promised.

The Fish
You see it in the river you make with a person in just
one look
from the other side of the room
and that corner of the eye
whose endowed purpose is to signal the beginning of a
smile.
Let us tie our mouths together, you say,
so we are not fossilized in the flip of the calendar or the
lilt of foreign lights
but found in the peace of an impromptu sidewalk
prayer circle
or that fleeting sliver of night found behind the clock's
searching hand.

Luisa Banchoff, Grade 12
Washington Lee High School
Arlington, VA
Poetry, Gold Key

contagion

I saw that
       smile
on your face
the corners of your mouth
stretching from ear to ear
and I just thought
you should know that I
       smiled
too
and when I went to my room
I thought it was funny
how our emotions
were interconnected
so I
       smiled
again

but then I heard
the vase crashing
your skull crushing
against a table
your bones crying
I heard your heartbeat
his enraged voice
the chair collapsing
his knuckles cracking
I heard it all
even when he broke down
into tears
his somber voice saying
"I'm sorry"

and just like always
you took him into your arms
caressed his cheek
while he looked into your swollen eyes
and touched your bruised face
he always says
"how could I have done this to you?"
and you say
"it was my fault"
except this time
I only wish
you could have spoken

I found out when
I heard him leave the house
and I walked down the stairs
to find your lifeless body
with a huge and overwhelming
        smile
on your face
I knew you were relieved
that he was finally gone
and since a
        smile
is contagious
 I couldn't help but
        smile
too.

Simran Batra, Grade 10
Robert E. Lee High School
Springfield, VA
Poetry, Honorable Mention

lost moments
(excerpted)

I picked up a picture taken long ago, in a different century with people whose lives were loss with the beauty of the innocent Afghanistan I had come to know and adore. The photograph brought me to my knees, taken in only the colors that were familiar to them; this black-and-white picture brought me to tears. It showed a fonder memory of mine: my dad, mom, my siblings, and I in a safer and happy environment. The camera captured us so well; me sitting on my dad's lap with the biggest smile on my face that portrayed the emotions I felt then: happiness, joy, excitement, and most of all love. My three sisters huddled together, playfully fighting, and my mom staring at my dad; her eyes showed an emotion so blissful and heavenly that I'd almost forgotten she could feel. So serene and calm we all looked back then in that one moment where I swear we looked completed.

I remembered: me at age two learning simple fragments of the language of Pashto, the origins of my ancestry buried with the dusts and debris of the coming war. These coherent words and new profound culture I was raised in kindred within me a feeling of nostalgia for a country I hoped I'd one day learn to love and accept. A feeling I'd understand years later in a different era, a more complicated part of the world.

This picture reminded me of moments from the past. Me at a park with my dad, us walking along the streets of Kandahar. Flash forward to me at the age of five with pigtails, when my family went to the mosque to pray for the safe comfort of our homes to last for eternity.

As I stared at this picture, I suddenly felt a desperate need to cry because this wasn't how anything was anymore. This little girl in Afghanistan wasn't the girl I was today. The world had changed and time had transformed me into a different person, too. That happy family that I longed for, that was captured in a simple picture, was long gone with the safety of Afghanistan. War had broken loose, blood and violence was everywhere, it took my dad and others as its token of victory, made me crippled at the age of six. This feeling of loneliness I felt every day would be with me throughout the journey of me discovering myself and my place in the world.

My dad's death had made my mother realize that Afghanistan wasn't our haven anymore, so we moved on to a place that seemed much safer, to get away from the memories of gunshots, of nightmares that kept us all awake at the longest hours of the night. We moved on to a new chapter in our life, to America: the country of freedom and the perfect abode of escape. It is here I discovered things, desires that could lead me to become a better version of myself. I could be an Interior Designer with my abilities to rearrange simple things into beautiful creations. I could even be something as simple as a Flight Attendant and just travel to unknown places in the world and help people. Living in the United States and growing up in Virginia made me forget the terrible memories I had in Afghanistan. It let me rediscover myself as a person, as my own separate being.

But as some memories were forgotten, others were deeply engraved into my heart. As Jamie Ford said, "I try not to live in the past, he thought, but who knows, sometimes the past lives in me." And in those few minutes that I had taken to stare at that picture I realized I wasn't in the present or the future, I was stuck in the past. I was trapped in memories of my father getting shot over and over again. It replayed in my head so vividly.

The morning of July 14, 1999, it was a sunny day, the birds were softly singing and the call for *athzan* could be heard all through the streets of Kandahar. My father looked happy that day, rushing around the house looking for his shoes so that he could be early to offer his prayer. He kissed my brother on his forehead and told my mom, "Don't wait up for me, I might be late." Those words until this day haunt me. Did he know he was going to die that day and had he accepted it, ready to go back to the Lord's house?

He left the house, trudging his shoes softly against the hard ground beneath his feet. He walked and walked and finally turned back once, like he was taking in all he was going to leave behind, and then just walked out the door. A shot was heard just after his departure, our present and future intermingled in that one incident.

Only a few years later, when I was around seven and I had matured, did my mom tell me what happened that morning. A few men who were assassins had come to kill Hamid Karzai's father and, thinking that my father was him, those men had unknowingly murdered my father in cold blood.

I shook my head and was back to the present, back to where my present self was. My mom walked in to the room looking around at the new environment I called my home. Everything was hidden in darkness: clothes neatly piled, books shelved, and, if you stared closely, you could make out the outline of my bed. To any stranger it may look as if no one lived in this room; there was no personal touch or homey aura, just a cold bleak air of perfume that was sprayed long ago, its smell barely left. My mom walked to me and asked what was wrong. I looked up and noticed I had moved from my bed and was sitting near my dresser. I could feel tears waiting to fall down, my clothes were crumpled, and I felt shaken up. After seeing the picture in my hand my mom sighed and shut the door softly behind her, letting me know she had left; the conversation was over. She along with the others had told me numerous times that he wasn't coming back and said to let the past go.

But I just couldn't; my past was haunting me in my nightmares and it was beckoning me to do something, like have an 'aha' moment. I just couldn't let my past go, so I picked myself up, holding the photo tightly in the palm of my hand, and walked to the bathroom.

Wrinkles and bags were defining my once young and joyful face; I wiped my face, letting the water do its task. The moment of realization came in just the perfect moment when I felt like giving up. I grabbed the photo, hurried out of the bathroom, left it under my pillow, and stopped. I stopped at my room door, fingers on the knob, and just took a moment to collect myself like the many times I had done before. The door was keeping me safe from the judgmental world outside where everything was in color; where things were in constant motion and feelings of the past could not take up space. I turned the knob of my room door slowly and stepped foot into my own realistic nightmare, allowing the past to patiently wait in my room to catch up with me later. I smiled at my mother, and everyone else that was a part of my present family, and took my place at the dining table, letting the story resume and the intermission end. The play was set into motion and all the characters had arrived.

Mari Baz, Grade 12
Hayfield Secondary School
Alexandria, VA
Personal Essay, Silver Key

spilled milk

When Ryan sees the Clorox bottles, he grips his mouth firmly with his hands and screams. The sound reverberates against the lifelines in his palms and vibrates his tongue.

When he's done screaming, he picks up the phone, dials Amalia's number, and leaves her a voicemail.

"Amalia," he says, struggling to keep his voice calm in the way an animal trainer would struggle to hold back an angry lion. "Something bad has happened. Call me as soon as possible."

Today

Beth's fingers wrap around Cynthia's thumb like a ring. Beth smells of milk and Jergen's Baby Oil and simplicity. She's got tiny lips that purse before she cries. Cynthia wonders why there are thousands of people worldwide searching for meaning in pieces of art in European countrysides when the most beautiful masterpiece you could ever find is right there in her arms.

"Who does Mommy love? Who does Mommy love?" Cynthia coos into Beth's ear. "It's you, baby, it's you!"

Yesterday

Ryan has endured the same routine every day for eight years.

He arrives at work at 8:35 a.m., a reasonable hour. He comes bearing his wife's piss-poor excuse for coffee and grits his teeth as he downs the last sip. He throws the cup away in the green trash can by the front entrance of the milk factory.

His job is simple: pour the unpasteurized milk through the narrow tube that protrudes from the forehead of the Milk Machine. The Milk Machine, of course, is a mostly self-sustaining monster comprised of exactly forty silvery, spinning parts. It is about the same length as the first floor of his townhouse, but it is only about two meters tall. The only thing it cannot do is pour the unpasteurized milk into itself. That is Ryan's job.

Ryan has no co-workers. The only person he sees regularly at the factory is Jeffrey, the owner, who comes in three days a week to make phone calls in his office. The two are friends, although they rarely speak.

Every morning Ryan sits, knee-deep in the aggressive silence that hides beneath the whirring of the Milk Machine. He is alone. He has been doing this for eight years. He pours and pours and pours the unpasteurized milk. There are full carts just waiting for Ryan's gentle touch, his calm aptitude. The final product is Ohio's Finest Milk, shipped out every night at six without fail.

He drives home in his clunky Buick, sliding easily through the gray six o'clock light, and thinks of his baby's hands reaching up for him. He often drives a little too quickly. Sometimes, he stops by Daisy's Supermarket, gets groceries for the family and a chocolate bar for himself. He always buys milk. He always doesn't want to.

There are some days that Ryan does not want to open his eyes and face another day of the loneliest job in Ohio. There are some days that he feels like the scent of unpasteurized milk has sifted from the surface of the carts and sunken into his brain. He is only calm when he thinks of his baby, Beth.

Today

After Jeffrey leaves Amalia the voicemail, he realizes this is a situation that deserves a face-to-face conversation. He knows the way to Amalia's office like the back of his hand.

He scrambles down the stairs, knocking his hip on the side of the Milk Machine as he makes his way outside. In the parking lot, the sun is expanding across the horizon, spreading its honey-golden rays across the mountains, hugging the clouds.

People are going to die watching this sunset.

When Jeffrey closes his eyes, going 90 miles per hour on a 75 miles per hour road, all he can see is milk.

Today

Beth's lips are starting to purse. Cynthia frowns, her nose against her baby's cheek, as pink and flushed as an unfolding rose.

"Don't cry, sweetheart," she whispers. "You hungry?"

Cynthia lifts herself up from the chair, still unsteady beneath the extra baby weight, and makes her way to the refrigerator door.

Yesterday

"Every day for eight years," Ryan is whispering, looking down at his lap. His hands ball into fists on his thighs. "I've been doing this every day for eight years."

"Ryan, you'll find a new job," Jeffrey says, and reaches out to touch him. Ryan shivers away from his fingertips and catches his bottom lip with his two front teeth.

"You don't understand." He looks up. There is a new look burning there, around the rims of his tear-studded eyes. He has fallen in love with his routine in the same way a lion at a zoo would fall in love with its cage. It is a dark and obsessive adoration; a dependence that he cannot shake. "This is my job. There is no other job for me."

"I'm sorry. I hope that we can get through this eventually." Jeffrey begins to rearrange papers on his desk, flattening their corners. "Maybe we can get a beer sometime soon."

Calmly, Ryan stands and extends his hand.

Ryan looks right through Jeffrey and says, "You're my pal, no matter what."

Today

"Amalia," Jeffrey grunts as he scrambles through her office door. The sweat beads down his face in rivulets, like condensation on the sides of the milk bottles. "I've got something to tell you."

What he should say is, "People are going to die." What he needs to say is, "I made a terrible mistake."

What he says is, "I think I need a glass of water."

Going down, the Aquafina will feel like two percent skim.

Today

"Your milk is almost ready," sings Cynthia, watching the Christmas mug circle the microwave, the milk basking and bubbling in the artificial light. Around and around and around.

There is something about this moment that makes her miss Ryan. She flips open her phone and dials his number. It rings.

Yesterday

Clorox. Every day for eight years, Ryan has passed by these same gallons of Clorox and never noticed them. Now this bleach is more beautiful to him than any routine; unmatched by the whir of the Milk Machine, the image of his baby's hands reaching up for him through the gray light, the memory of his wife's bowtie lips beneath her veil.

He gathers the first bottle in his hands and handles it cautiously as he climbs the stairs.

Peering down the narrow tube, Ryan softly smiles, his lips pursing gently. He considers the scent of unpasteurized milk. He considers the taste of milk fresh out of the carton. As he untwists the cap to the Clorox, he begins to read the warning label aloud to himself.

Today

"I don't fully understand." Amalia usually has green eyes but today lightning shocks across her dilated pupils. Her fingers are pressed so deeply into her forehead that Jeffrey worries they will leave scars.

"We have to deal with this. You have to tell me how to deal with this."

To calm herself, Amalia looks down at the certificate on her desk, her only recorded thank you for being an Exceptional Food Safety Agent. "Let me just—assess the situation again. Okay? Tell me to stop when I've got something wrong."

"Okay."

"Five gallons of Clorox bleach were poured into the Milk Machine. Five."

"Yes."

"Five gallons of Clorox bleach were pasteurized along with five gallons of milk, poured into bottles, and shipped to Daisy's supermarket."

"Yes."

"This happened yesterday, and by now, all five gallons have been bought."

"Yes."

The ensuing silence is as loud as an atomic bomb. Finally, Amalia sits, the weight of her body sagging into the chair cushions. She cups her face with her hands. She curses. They reach for each other at the same time.

Yesterday

Ryan drinks and drinks.
He begins to look tired.

Today

Beth's little lips nibble at the baby bottle before she begins to drink. When she finally does, tranquility settles over her pristine blue eyes.

She begins to look very tired.

Emily Birnbaum, Grade 11
Winston Churchill High School
Potomac, MD
Short Story, Gold Key

breaking away

I used to love thunderstorms. I would sit for hours with my tiny face pressed against the cold glass windowpane, mesmerized by the bright flashes of lightning, watching intently as they split the horizon in half. I loved to hear the rain tapping on my roof, to watch the drops race down my window and plummet to the ground. I loved the suspense of waiting for the thunder to shatter the sky, echoing as its deafening roar drowned out all other sounds. My favorite part, however, was the silence; the stillness after the storm had passed, when the rain dripped from the tree branches, and the saturated ground squished under my feet. Now even the thought of a storm leaves me paralyzed with fear, unable to think or move, only to relive my most terrifying day again and again.

"Kaylie, c'mon!" Clara grabbed my hand, dragging me out of my house. We had been neighbors since birth, practically sisters. We skipped down the dirt path, carrying a soccer ball, and dust kicked up behind our heels and left a brown cloud in the distance. We ran, following the winding dirt road, bordered on both sides by acres of corn fields. A cool breeze moved the dry leaves, sending a whisper through the fields. We stopped running at a small, barely noticeable path in one of the corn fields. To the right of the path was a worn, handmade sign that read: "Clara and Kaylie's Secret Passage." The sign was weathered and decaying, almost illegible, the result of nearly seven years in the open Nebraska air.

Clara and I turned down the path, just as we had done hundreds of times before. We ducked under head-high corn stalks, and wove in and out of the yellowing leaves, following the narrow, winding path through the field. We knew every turn by heart—for we came down this path every day—but we were still amazed to see what lay at the end.

The bright green of the grass contrasted with the neutral grays and browns of the corn field, and the cloudy sky seemed to part right above the clearing. It was a soccer field. Two goals sat on opposite ends of the fields. The crossbar of one goal was slanted, and the opposing goal had a hole in the net, but neither looked old. They looked loved. And they were.

Our goals had been in this field since before Clara and I could even walk. Our parents used to bring us out here and watch as we crawled around on the lush, soft grass. They would smile as they saw the looks of pure happiness on our faces. Years passed, but even as we grew up, those expressions did not change. This field was our treasure. It inspired us not only to want to play soccer, but also to make something of ourselves. No one from our families had ever gone to college, and none of our parents had ever even left Nebraska. People said that soccer was our ticket out. It could get us scholarships to college; it could open up opportunities that otherwise never would have been possible. And we believed them.

Maybe it could have happened. Maybe all of our dreams would have come true, but they didn't. Instead, one second changed the rest of my life forever.

"…And Kaylie shoots, and scores!" Clara laughed as she pretended to announce the winning goal of a championship game.

Dark gray clouds were rolling above us. The wind had picked up, and our hair was swirling in halos above our heads, but neither of us paid attention. We chased each other around and around the field, like we always did. We barely noticed when the first raindrop landed. We were oblivious to our surroundings until it started pouring. Buckets and buckets of rain dumped on our heads. We screamed, laughing as we ran for cover, but we were in the middle of an open field with nowhere to hide. Clara grabbed my hand and pulled me onto the field. We stared up at the sky, watching thousands of raindrops descend from the clouds. I spun in circles, feeling like I was the center of the storm, as Clara cartwheeled through the water. Suddenly a bright streak of lightning flashed over the corn fields, and seconds later a deafening crack of thunder broke through the sky. We weren't afraid. We watched the lightning once more before resuming our game.

We were back in our championship match. I passed the ball to Clara as she ran up the sideline. She dribbled towards the goal and slowed down as she pulled her foot back to shoot the winning goal.

It only took a millisecond. Faster than the blink of an eye, a bolt of lightning shot from the sky. Striking only feet away from me, I could feel the heat. I could hear the crackling of electricity. My hair stood on end. My eyes shut, but when I opened them, I saw something that made my heart stop. Clara, standing only a few yards away from me, was glowing. A halo of yellow light radiated from her skin. In slow motion she was lifted from the ground, before being roughly thrown back to the earth. She landed limply, and the world spun.

It has been five years. Five years without my best

friend. Five years without soccer. Five years without our field. I haven't touched a soccer ball since the accident. I shut everything that could trigger the memory out of my life.

Today is the fifth anniversary of her death. I walk down the dirt road slowly, remembering five years ago today. Alone, I follow the winding road, carrying only a soccer ball. I turn at our path. Our sign has long since disappeared. I push past corn stalks that no longer tower over my head. I still know every turn by heart, even though I haven't visited the path in years. The narrow passage opens into a field, taking my breath away once again. Tears stream down my face as I stand by the sideline. I hear Clara's laugh. She was never afraid, and I shouldn't be either. Knowing she would want me to do this, I step onto the field. Images flit before my eyes. Memories I tried for years to suppress come flooding back. I see us growing up together, and I remember every day so clearly. I drop the ball in front of the goal and pull my foot back, ready to shoot. I strike the ball and watch as it soars into the goal, breaking away from my fear forever.

Kelsey Bowen, Grade 8
The Potomac School
McLean, VA
Flash Fiction, Gold Key

down under
(excerpted)

Donn was 13 years old and had never seen the sky. He'd seen pictures, of course, and heard stories, but he'd also heard they were nothing compared to the real thing. If he had been born above, things would be different. He'd always have enough to eat, he'd live in a house with more than three rooms, and he'd be able to save his parents. Donn remembered the first day they found out. The day his parents hit stage one.

It had started out as a normal dinner, swamp vines and carp, with his parents pressuring him to get a job.

"You are thirteen already! Pick a career!" his dad had said loudly. Donn could hear the barely repressed anger. He ignored him.

"Can we have something else to eat, Mom? Like skunk or ducks?" Donn asked.

"You know how expensive those are," she replied. "Practically Upper food."

"So? We deserve Upp-" Donn was interrupted by a loud scream. His head shot around to see his father doubled over in pain, his pale face twitching and his body writhing on the floor. Suddenly he stopped, his eyes blank, his arms relaxed.

"No," Donn whispered. "No." He stared, transfixed, as blood dripped from his father's ears.

Everyone Down Under knew two things about the Plague: one, there were six stages (seizures/blood overflow, twitching, migraines, cracked skin, dementia, and, finally, death); and two, there was no cure. At least, no cure Down Under. Donn had heard rumors, rumors of hunting parties and raids that go Up. If he could get that cure, he could save his parents. Which was exactly why he was in Down West, the seediest part of the Cavern.

Every time Donn came into the Cavern, he was amazed. Growing up in the Tunnels, the massive, octagonal cavern topped off with a half sphere seemed massive, and with a population of 20,000,000, it was. Even more amazing was the fact that it was all carved out of the same stone, a 100-square-mile deposit of limestone carved out by Uppers before they took over the surface and sent the poor below. The Cavern was the capital of The Lower Republic of Australia (more popularly referred to as Down Under), almost perfectly mirroring the city of Sydney no more than 100 yards above. The tall stone towers reached up to 75 stories tall, eternally struggling to break the surface.

The Cavern was the first city built Down Under, meant to be the solution to extreme overpopulation. But it was a solution only beneficial to the rich: send the unseen, unheard, underside of the people to a place they would never hear of again, hundreds of feet below the surface. However, once free to do as they pleased underground, they enacted the only form of rebellion they could: expansion. By the time Donn was born, there were thousands of towns and cities, all connected by tunnels, the highways of the underground.

"Hey kid, got some spare visas?"

Donn turned to see an emaciated old man huddled in an alleyway, his skin a greenish hue and his eyes squinting, clear signs of a long-time swamp water addict. As Donn looked closer, he was alarmed to see that this was no old man but a young man no older than 17, his future ruined by the comforting fantasy that swamp water brought.

"No, sorry," he said as he hurried past.

Normally Donn would have gladly given him some change, but with his parents invalids right now and his brother gone for over a year, he could waste none. He looked around for the symbol of the rebellion, an arrow pointed towards the surface. If anyone would know how to save parents, the Rebels would. According to rumor, the Rebels lived like kings, benefitting from their risky raids topside. Suddenly a voice rang out at him. "Well, what do we have here?"

Donn turned to see a group of pale (this coming from a boy who had never seen the sun) people in their mid-twenties, armed with spur-gloves and homemade clubs, coming his way. He forced a smile despite the dread in his stomach.

"H-hi. May I help you?" He heard a laugh behind him and was stunned to see he was surrounded. *How did that happen?* he wondered. The largest of the gang stepped forward. He was tall, wearing homemade black clothes. He would have stood out anyway due to his immense height (Donn guessed somewhere around 7 feet) but his hair color made it easy to point him out: a freakish red that contrasted with his pitch black skin with intricate spirals and pictographs shaved in.

"Sure, you can help us. Beat yourself up, and give us your money willingly. Makes our job much easier." The man spoke with a strange accent, one Donn had never heard before. He looked around, searching for an escape, but found none. He resigned to defeat and reached into his pocket to pull out his wallet. Don tossed it into the man's hands and felt the hopes of saving his parents disappear. He studied the ground until he heard the man cough. He looked up to see the man. (Ares, according to the tattoo on his biceps.)

"This isn't enough," he said.

Donn felt his blood run cold. "What do you mean? It's all I have. It has to be enough!" He felt the cold sting of Ares' hand hit his face.

"Are you saying I'm a liar?" Ares glared at him with a stare that could make full-grown men cower and cry. Suddenly Donn realized it didn't matter what he did. Ares was a psycho and he was about to be slaughtered. This hunch was confirmed when he saw the gleam in his eye as Ares stepped forward, his club raised like a lumberjack about to strike. Donn saw it swing towards his head and he closed his eyes, bracing himself for the unavoidable impact. He was shocked to realize it never came. Cautiously he opened his eyes. He looked up to see Ares on the ground, a hulking mass of muscle standing above him.

"What the swur are you doing?!" the man screamed at him.

"He was a threat to the House!" Ares whimpered. Donn was stunned to see the man who only moments before had been a terrifying giant rendered useless.

"This puny kid? Get up! You're done, back to drone!" He then turned to Donn "Sorry, he doesn't represent us all. My name is Mero. I'm the second in command of this Rebel Hive. Either join us, or leave the city and don't come back."

It took Donn a moment for him to process this. These ruthless thugs were Rebels? Why would Ares be an authority figure?

"Hey kid, either come or leave."

Donn hesitated, and then rushed after them.

Leo Canty, Grade 7
Alice Deal Middle School / Writopia Lab
Washington, DC
Short Story, Silver Key

silent
(excerpted)

On Monday morning, Karim stopped by to let me know about the raid on the university the previous evening. A group of police officers and members of the Basij raided the dormitories, looking to punish students who had been protesting election results.

"It was two or three of them against one of us. They dragged us across the ground," he described, "and forced us into submission." Then Karim pulled up his shirt.

I gasped.

Rows upon rows of bruises and cuts ravaged his chest. Hot red, splotchy, and angry marks where they had kicked and beaten him.

His beautiful skin was marred.

"We need to do something," I said, touching one of Karim's unbroken wounds gently. "They can't just get away with this!"

"Some of us decided to join the group of protesters along Azadi Street," Karim said, grabbing my hand tightly. There was a fire in his eyes that I had never seen before. "Nasrin, you should come."

I was dumbstruck. *A protest — how could I even contribute?*

But after looking at his skin, I made my decision. The cruel marks represented not only the horrible injustice that had been brought upon the students, but the injustice brought upon the entirety of the *Iranian people*. What kind of government would allow this kind of atrocity?

"Yes." I finally nodded. "I'm in."

We sprinted down three blocks to reach Azadi Street, where a deafening jubilance filled the air as thousands marched in protest of the election results. Decked in green shirts, hats, and bandanas, they walked together, raising two fingers in a gesture of peace. They held flags, balloons, and banners, calling out, "The election was fake! Recount the votes!" Others handed green bandanas and scarves to any passerby.

One woman handed Karim and me some green ribbon and hats. "Bless you," she yelled, trying to outperform the crowd. She clasped her hands over mine tightly. "Bless both of you." Then, she left to pass bandanas to other protesters.

Karim grabbed my wrist and tied the ribbon on. Then he slipped the cap over my hijab.

"Thanks."

He pointed to his ears, and mouthed, *I can't hear you.*

I laughed. Although we couldn't communicate properly, I felt the tangible excitement in the air.

Someone bumped into me, almost knocking me down. "Sorry," the man said, lumbering away with a giant poster board.

Suddenly, I realized that over half of the people were holding signs in protestation of the election. Some were printed on simple carbon paper, while others were written with thick, black markers.

"Ahmadinejad is NOT our president," one sign read. *"Solidarity,"* another called for.

There were many variations:

"Charge Ahmadinejad with fraud!"

"End dictatorship in Iran!"

"No more lies!"

"We want democracy!"

"Where is my vote?!" a soft, weak voice uttered.

Karim and I turned to find an elderly man, who was crying out in desperation. "Where is my vote?!" he croaked, shaking with rage. He waved his flimsy piece of cardboard around, as if the Guardian Council could hear him.

I watched in fascination at how such an old man, who was undeniably and helplessly drowned out by the other protesters much younger than he, never gave up. He repeated the question over and over.

"Where is my vote?! *Where is my vote?!*"

"Where is my vote?" I whispered to myself. Then I looked at Karim, who nodded.

"Where is my vote?" I said louder.

"Where is my vote?!" Karim joined me. He grabbed me by the arm and pulled me into the throng with him. "Where is my vote?!"

The people around us started to pay attention and joined us in unison, chanting the question over and over.

"Where is my vote?! Where is my vote?!"

The choir of voices grew into a crescendo, growing louder and louder and louder – until we became one body, one people, *one voice*.

I tasted freedom.

On that day in the middle of Azadi Street, I had never felt more proud to be an Iranian citizen.

I just hoped they could hear us at the Sa'dabad Palace.

* * *

Something was different the next Saturday when I arrived. There was no singing and no merriness. No jeers at the government, or shouts of "Where's my vote?" Instead, an ominous tension penetrated the air.

I caught up with Karim at our usual spot and handed him a sign. "What's going on?"

He pointed to a large assembly of men, armed and dressed in police gear, marching towards the other protesters. An officer with a megaphone shouted, "Go home! Go home, or face the consequences!"

Suddenly, a shot rang out.

Screams pierced the air as the crowd panicked. People dashed in every direction, trying to flee the scene. Women were crying and men were shouting as police surged towards a crowd that gathered at the end of the block.

Karim ran towards the commotion, and I followed. We found several men surrounding a young woman, lying on the ground, and my mouth fell open in shock.

Blood spilled out of her chest and ran between her fingers as she clutched her shirt. Her eyes remained wide open, and blood soon poured from her eyes, nose, and mouth, soaking her skin.

Blood red.

"Neda!" one man screamed, collapsing next to her. "Oh please!"

"Let's move," Karim suggested, his voice wavering.

We ran down the block, only to be greeted by billowing smoke. Alarms wailed. Cars baked in flames. But the worst was the anguished pleas of those rounded up and subdued by hundreds police forces. "I'll do anything! Please! Don't hurt them!"

"We have to get out of here!" I yelled. "They-- AHH!" I shrieked as a pair of strong hands trapped me, fingers grappling my neck.

"Let her go!" Karim lunged at us.

I screamed.

Two officers snuck up behind Karim and twisted him between them.

Struggling futilely against the man who held me, I watched in horror as they shoved Karim onto his back and drove punches into his stomach and groin. Karim gasped in pain, tears streaming down his face.

Our eyes met for a single moment. *I'm sorry,* he mouthed.

One of our assailants saw this and crushed his skull beneath his boot. Then they dragged him away.

I never saw Karim again.

Brittany Cheng, Grade 12
Montgomery Blair High School
Silver Spring, MD
Short Story, Gold Key

the certainty of a personal hell

my sanity is
an idealist, a dry sponge,
a cup of tea at 2:30 in the morning,
a vacuum for those afternoons when I wake up
with Starburst wrappers stuck to my cheek
after falling asleep past the small hours of the night
staying up watching 30 Rock and playing solitaire.

it is a text message from someone saying "how are you"
not "goodbye" or "sorry it had to go down like this"
it is the sounds of Belle & Sebastian and terrible
Korean pop
in an otherwise silent and empty household on
Wednesday.

my sanity: it's not the best, but it's there,
it's not one to put up much of a fight
it runs away at the first rumble of thunder,
like it owes the storm money
it cowers until the aftermath
then assumes a holier-than-thou attitude
like it knew the right thing to do the entire time
it just didn't bother to do it.

"we'll get through this," it says
I say, "how can we, if I don't know what 'this' is?"
"we are tough as nails," it says
but nails are always either rusty
or crusty with toe jamb and they chip easily.

I look down at the small clear plastic pill
holding the green grainy flowers
like it could be either holy water or cyanide
my sanity, it says it's "sure as hell" about this
but is hell really that certain?

Helena Chung, Grade 12
Chantilly High School
Chantilly, VA
Poetry, Gold Key

sometimes

Sometimes I think about love,
And what it means, and what it is.
I think that somewhere out there,
Someone is standing around,
And one day they will love me.
But could they?
Could they love all of me?

My old books, covered in dust but never forgotten,
The pictures of friends taped to my mirror.
The guitar in the corner never put away in the case,
The sweatshirt tossed to the ground carelessly.
The stacks of journals I will always leave blank,
Because I find something beautiful in leaving them
untouched.

Could someone love me?

My adoration for hot chocolate and plaid woolen
blankets,
The words I whisper in the dark so I can be sure no
one will hear.
The scar on my wrist, cut by a glass cup when I was a
child,
My worn out shoes covered in dirt that I keep in my
closet.
The old white blanket with the black mascara stains,
From the night I cried and didn't remove my make-up.

Could anyone really, really love me?

The loneliness that often threatens to swallow me whole,
Those nights I'm far too tired for sleep.
All the painful memories scarred in my mind,
The moments when I get so scared I cannot breathe.
Dozens of stories I keep saved on my computer – my feelings,
The sort of writing I can never share with anyone.

There is someone out there playing their favorite sport,
Or groaning at the thought of homework,
And I've been told one day this person will love me.
But how could they?

How could they love a girl like me,
When I cannot even love myself most days?
How could someone accept my outward flaws,
Along with the secret ones I keep to myself?

Sometimes I think about love,
And I wonder if, like most things,
I will be the forgotten one,
And no one else will really care.

Sometimes I think about what's real and what isn't,
Sometimes I think about love.

And I always end up thinking about you.

Katie Coble, Grade 9
Yorktown High School
Arlington, VA
Poetry, Honorable Mention

white-out

I burned my thumb. A half-moon
on the underside, achingly pink
as if my blood had swooned in the oven.
The doctors had no idea
why fabric scorched skin.
"You were so
careful," they marveled, turning
my thumb back and forth, bending it until
the skin turned white. Then, satisfied,
they had me wrap it in gauze, tightly,
tightlytightlytightlytightlytightly--
now, *that's* more like it.
That winter, I learned the true way
to get better: tie yourself into a knot,
then
suffocate.

Small talk: "What happened
to you?
I mean, what happened to your thumb?"
Oh, this? Nothing much—I wasn't
looking, not seeing
what I should have: an oven mitt
too attracted to the flame.
Weeks pass
before snow falls. Rain washes it away.

A word for the time when
we have no other words:
My teeth grind it, and terror becomes
Tear her.

The snow comes back. Nature, running
its course: a phrase we have for the phenomenon
of inevitability.

My hands are sunsets, the tips oozing
with royalty, the nails a cool, distant
blue, and of course, the incomparable
pink thumb crowned in white.
I'm so alive,
I'm practically the tides.

My back fights with mountains
to own ridges.
I win. I do not
know how to feel about this victory.
My ribs keep me
awake, poking and punctuating the rise and fall
of my breath.

I swallow
symbols. I see them
everywhere: what is on that plate, what is
in that bowl. I am conducting the world's
experiment:
how many flakes of
a person can fit into one tablespoon
before they spill over
the edge?

One tablespoon is too large.
I use smaller and smaller
spoons: a half, a quarter, an eighth— until
my hands are nothing but fistfuls
of spoons, palms of silver.

I have never excelled
in mathematics, but dear God, am I
trying.

Here is trying:
a rib cage jutting through skin,
a hand on a hipbone,
open eyes and closed windows.
Here is trying:
a fist in a hysterical mouth,
a hand on a hysterical heart,
low blood pressure and melting snow.
Here is trying:
knees as round as oranges
about to drop, about to stain my feet.
Three words, three ways to lie
about
the grains of dust
in the measuring spoons. I can see myself;
I press my palms of silver
against my eyes. I do not want
to know.

Sarah Cooke, Grade 12
Sidwell Friends School / Writopia Lab
Washington, DC
Poetry, Gold Key

abandoned storms
(excerpted)

He must be somewhere out there, and even if he's not, then someone must be. I can't be the only person left in the world. I can't.

I walk along the sidewalk, through the empty city. Shards of glass blanket the road, creating a deceptive shimmering surface. The buildings, many of them reduced to piles of concrete and twisted metal, glare down at me as I pass. A row of street lights line the road, though only one still carries electricity. As I walk underneath it, the light flickers, and then dies.

I hear the crunch of footsteps on glass behind me, and whirl around. There is no one there. I stop and listen hard, but now the only sound is that of the wind, a soft, almost imperceptible whisper that comes and goes as it pleases. The city is empty now; no more honking cars or bustling people, no more bright lights. So what was that sound?

I shake my head and continue walking, telling myself that I must be imagining things. I once heard that being alone for a long time can do that sort of thing. I pause at an intersection, closing my eyes as memories of the past come flooding in.

I continue to walk, my mind stuck thinking about everything I have lost. Everything that led up to this wasteland.

"A second tsunami devastates Shanghai...Mysterious sickness kills twenty in Easton, Connecticut, reports of disease spreading beyond the east coast...Another round of American troops

deployed to Japan...Citizens warned to stay off streets...high threat of another air raid..."

Every day I would turn on the television, hoping for something other than disaster after disaster. Eventually I ignored the TV altogether. Life went on like that for a while. People tried to go about their lives like nothing was happening, but the evidence was everywhere. You could see it in the newspapers, and in the lines on people's faces. The war couldn't be forgotten for long.

Meanwhile, the weather got stranger and stranger. Some places were plagued with storms, while others suffered through months of drought. My city was one of the places with the storms. In the summertime, the sound of rain beating on the pavement and thunder shaking the sky replaced the chirping of crickets and birdsong. In the winter, we grew used to snow-covered streets and the many, many days off from school. We grew used to shivering in our apartments and had a stock of candles at the ready in the case of a power outage. We grew used to getting by and not complaining. We tried to convince ourselves that because we still had a home, and we were still alive, we should be happy.

Suddenly, a ship appeared on the island, full of soldiers. Another ship arrived with supplies. Within a week, construction of oil rigs and pipelines had begun. About a month later, one of the oil rigs got blown up. And then the war began.

The U.S. backed Japan. Countries chose sides. Some weren't even fighting for the same things, but they fought all the same. The war spread everywhere, wreaking havoc and ruining lives.

There seemed to be one unspoken rule. No countries touched their nuclear weapons. I guess it was deterrence, the assumption that if one country used their bombs, the others would in retaliation. And people had heard enough theories of the apocalypse, or maybe it was common sense, to know that a nuclear war would wipe out most of the human race.

Even so, there was one day that I remember more than anything else from before. It was the day the war entered directly into my life. It was the end of my old life.

"Day, are you paying attention?" my teacher called. Obviously not. My eyes scanned the board, trying to work out an answer.

"Yeah, um..." The sound of a siren cut through the air, and the fire alarm above our door began to flash red. There was a cringe-inducing whine, like the sound a microphone makes when you swing it around, then a voice crackled on the school intercom.

"All students go to the nearest designated emergency shelter. This is not a drill. All students..."

At least a hundred of us had crammed into that shelter in the basement of the school. My friend, Jace, had made his way through the room, coming to stand beside me. Jace's baseball cap, showing his support for the Yankees, was tilted to the side. It looked like it was going to fall off his head.

The alarmingly loud chirp of a cricket breaks the silence. I stop short, and step on something on the sidewalk. I pick it up, turning it over in my hands. It's a navy blue baseball cap. Although the brim is worn and dirty, I can still see the once white letters on the front. The symbol of the New York Yankees.

"So," Jace said. He had taken off his cap and was twisting it in his hands. "When do you think we'll get out of here?"

"Who knows," I replied. "An air raid like this could last all night."

That day in the school basement was the last day things were even close to normal.

I stare at the baseball cap in my hands. Is it Jace's, the very same one from that day all those years ago? It could be. It wasn't always here, or I would have found it, right? I walk these streets often enough.

I try to quell my rising hope, knowing that this will most likely end in disappointment. But my heart is beating quickly, as the thoughts in my head go wild. *Someone's here. Him? Must be. He's alive!*

I can hear the cry of seagulls and the faintest rushing of water. The wind has picked up now, just enough to blow my hair across my face.

"Time to go," I mutter to myself. I walk with a purpose, heading back towards the edge of the city. I do not stop until I am in front of what's left of a cafe that I used to go to with my parents. I walk around to the side of the building, and slip in through the hole in the wall.

When I first came by here, so long ago, the door was locked, though some of the higher windows were smashed. After some searching, I found a hole in the wall that led to one of the back rooms of the restaurant. I have since swept up the glass and barricaded the door, making sure that no one can use the entrance from the street and catch me unaware. Not that it ever made much of a difference. When Jace left, there was no one left besides me. There was no one left to hide from, just as until now, there has been no one left to find.

My mind begins to wander as it often does on days like this. Why am I still here, still living in this forsaken place? Are there countries still out there, cities still thriving, still bright and noisy with light and life? It used to be that you could go on the Internet, or turn on the TV, or the radio, and be almost instantly connected to anywhere you chose. I could go to the telephone and dial a number, and be able to talk to someone on the other side of the world.

Now, though, I have purpose again. A purpose beyond just survival. If Jace is alive—and I have reason again to hope that he is—I will find him.

Mina Cooper, Grade 8
The Potomac School / Writopia Lab
McLean, VA
Short Story, Silver Key

this girl's life
(excerpted)

2001.

There is a girl who at the age of five receives the biggest shock of her life. She is in recess, in both spirit and in school. Free of mind and of the classroom. Inside, teachers rearrange their rooms; they are oblivious to the real countenance of students and the faces they share amongst each other. A boy approaches the girl. She does not know his name - he rarely ever shows up for school. He sits beside her on the bench, looks at her and then at her shoes before standing up to leave. He asks her why she is so slow, and when she does not respond, he rolls his eyes and runs towards the other kids, as if his aim was to rub the trail of his youthful energy in her face, as a tire may kick up dirt behind in its acceleration. She will be asked this very same question a number of times at school and will never know how to answer. She will never let on that the question almost always reduces her to tears.

The girl begins to realize the differences between her and the other kids, and how those differences informed who she is, or rather the lack of what she is supposed to be. A child and what a child means, someone full of energy, full of joy and curiosity. She cannot articulate these feelings, but from a very young age, she seemed to have a good understanding of the world, and her place in it, a skill that others her age did not acquire. She has paid for this talent with her limbs. She is cumbersome; she has never been as active as the kids that she attended school with; a game of tag leaves her heart verging on the edge of a cardiac arrest. Most times, she sits down next to the teachers at recess and avoids activity. Fun is something she has to work at, to work at ensuring that games of tag do not shudder to a halt whenever she is doing the chasing; as they almost always invariably do. She can hardly keep up, and in the eyes of the other children she is condemned. She reads their messages clearly. She is lazy. She is disappointing.

2003.

After taking her weight, height and blood pressure, Dr. Fisher calls her mother into another room. At this stage she does not mind these private conversations with Dr. Fisher. For a while she has had her suspicions that she is sick, but does not know how sick. While she waits, she plays with the stethoscope above the "Hazardous" bin even though she had been told not to. She pretends she is the doctor. Physician heal thyself.

Her mother and Dr. Fisher return. It is in this moment that she learns of her disability. She has arthritis. The word keeps buzzing around in her head for the longest time. She asks her mom plenty of questions. For a while she believes that she will end up dying from arthritis. When she tells her mother this, her mother laughs and explains that it is a bone disease causing damage to her joints. She understands why she has lived in so much pain for so long now but refuses to accept it.

2004.

She realizes that she is not a child. What child lives with pain as painful as this? She has been raised around adults. There are never any children around the neighborhood for her to play with, and she is an only child. By the time she hits the fourth grade, she is going to school with a cane. The girl is shattered by the thought of being the only nine-year old using a cane when other kids can run and flip down the halls. Often times she wants to ditch the cane in some desolate part of the school just to prevent the questions. But she knows that she really needs it to walk.

2005.

The girl begins to go to physical therapy. Dr. Fisher smiles and motions both her and her mother to a room at the rear of the hospital. She is told to remove her clothes and change into one of the white hospital gowns. She thinks of all the things that can go wrong. Her mom fills out the paperwork and places a reassuring hand on her daughter's shoulder.

By the time the doctor walks back in, she is relaxed. She is told to try to sit straight without the cane, to stand against the back wall and reach for her toes as far as she can. She cannot get past the top of her knee.

"Is there pain?" Dr. Fisher asks.

She nods her head. She brushes the sweat off of her forehead and continues to push farther. The girl imagines doing toe touches and push-ups like the cheerleaders at her school do. After many failed attempts to reach anything past her knees, she moves on to the next exercise. Her mother encourages her from across the room. Next, she must walk up and down a flight of six steps. The thought of possibly tripping and breaking a bone scares her. She manages to push through it and goes back and forth repeatedly. She is able to do this five times. Last time she came, she could only manage two. The girl is very proud of herself. She gives a half-smile to the doctor, turning away in happiness and shock.

As she re-dresses, the doctor suggests using Bengay every night on her trouble areas for thirty days. She says that it won't help all the time, but it will ease the pain a little. She isn't happy at all with the uncertainty of the doctor's words.

2007.

Middle school seems to fly by. The children are required to wear the school's white and blue uniform so it makes the girl feel a bit better about her scars. She can wear long sleeves and pants as much as she pleases without being asked any embarrassing questions. Most days the girl limps down the hallways.

"What's the matter?" A passerby asks.

"Nothing," she says.

She is not going to use that brown wooden cane for anything, except maybe to kill hard-to-reach insects. She despises that cane. She has blamed it for ruining her life as a kid. The girl knows that her arthritis was the cause of everything, but the cane added to humiliation. She never wants the cane to be there as a symbol of all the things she can't do. It is one thing to use it in elementary school where ignorant kids didn't know any better than to tease and mock. But middle school is a new kind of game for her. The girl refuses to be ridiculed and humiliated by kids that just don't understand.

2008-2012.

There is a young lady who realizes that she is no longer a disappointment to anyone. Not to her peers, or to her family. She is more confident in her appearance and wears clothing that flaunts the healing scars. She is full of energy and joy and actually doesn't mind walking long distances. The tender hellos and the sorrowful goodbyes she receives are all too eye-opening. Yes, arthritis is still her condition, but it has not damaged her. The young woman knows that she is not useless. She is cherished. She is cheerful. She is able.

Bridget Dease, Grade 12
Duke Ellington School of the Arts
Washington, DC
Personal Essay, Silver Key

immigrant

I. immigrant
I miss the fluid feel of my old name in my mouth, my tongue tracing
the soft syllables. It got stolen along the way somehow,
though I don't speak in broken English anymore. Add it to the list of items
we lost, but have to learn to stop missing.
Our bloodlines are still dragging,
those threads tangled vaguely in that space between east and west,
assigned identities not quite fitting. I know they said *the war is over,*
but I still want to fight.

II. american dream
I press my fingers against the pillow of my stomach, wishing I could feel something sharp,
hoping to find ridges of bone. My fingertips stray to my hips, and I pinch
at their softness, as if that could trim away the excess flesh. As if I could
rend my marrows apart, neat and surgical, along the seams of spine and thigh –
insides turned to spun dust, like the stuffing of a toy come undone.
I stare at the mirror and then the glossy five-page spread again, my heart aching
for a face pale as snowdrifts
and all-American blue eyes the size of saucers – the kind I wish I had,
set into the faces of blushing girls with gaps between

their thighs
and lemon-blond hair, beckoning to me from the
magazines.
Leaning in close to the mirror, I pull my eyelids wider,
pucker my lips, tug at my skin until it turns sore
in the hopes that this will make me beautiful.

III. daughter one
My mother was the one who taught me
how to turn my heart to stone. *Make your eyes dark like
bullet holes,* she whispers softly
while braiding my hair. *Set your mouth like a razorblade.
The war is not yet over.*
Of all the children, I was old enough to remember
the acrid tang of napalm, blooms of crimson on the
humid air,
the swelling flares of gunfire. I tell myself
to get used to the weight of that stone hanging heavy in
my chest.
They'd said I'd never be pretty here, so I want to
become beautiful instead –
but the terrible sort of beauty, the kind that makes men
die,
the kind that launches a thousand ships. I want a
revolution that brings up the blood.
A long time ago, I tore out the threads
fastened to my heart. There's electricity in my veins
that could burn cities to the ground.

Aline Dolinh, Grade 9
Oakton High School
Vienna, VA
Poetry, Gold Key and American Voices Nominee

toulouse
(excerpted)

There are these kids in Toulouse. They're on a school trip, on an exchange with some French kids. They're sitting in an art room making a collage out of massacred magazines. Their teachers watch them closely, and when the project is over, they are told to stay back.

The curtains are drawn shut. A teacher speaks. "You know how, last week, three soldiers were killed by a man on a motorcycle."

The kids nod. They heard about this, but they aren't scared. Those who are scared hide the fear with jokes; whenever they see a motorcycle, they fake scream, but they all know that they could never get hurt.

"Today, the man attacked a Jewish school. He killed four people." The teacher lets this hang for a minute. Then says, "We all stay here today." The kids are at a French school not ten blocks from the Jewish school. They were scheduled to go shopping today, in town. Now they stay in the school, under a grey sky, and wait.

There's this kid named Beatrice. She's borderline depressed, she's been bullied because she's smart, and she has the feeling that nobody likes her. In a few hours, the boy she loves will get a girlfriend.

She loves talking to him. About anything: books, movies, games, politics. Anything to take her mind off the killer. And his, too. When the teacher told them the news, he put his head in his hands and said nothing.

But when she talks with him, he laughs. He smiles. He opens up.

She loves seeing him. The other girls don't think he's handsome, but she sees a listener. She sees a thinker. The other boys tease him because he's an ice dancer. But she sees it as something beautiful, something different.

She wore a nicer shirt today. It's Monday, and she thought about him all weekend. She wanted to look nice. And she hangs out with him at lunch and in the schoolyard, after the killings have been announced, after it starts raining.

She's loved him since sixth grade, the start of middle school. It's eighth grade now, and she feels the same way. She has no classes with him, but she still thinks about him, and what it would be like if they were together. She thinks of it always, right before she goes to sleep.

There's this kid named Karl. He's a skater, he's teased because of it, and he is scared. The killer reminded him how short his life is. How he could die at any second. How he needs to make sure that he leaves no loose ends.

He's had two girlfriends. The first was in fifth grade: they would talk about books after they read the same ones. The second was in sixth grade. She moved, and broke up with him the day before. He wants a third. Not to collect a large number of girlfriends, but because there's this one he really likes. She's in a lot of his classes. She plays hard to get, but it's clear that she likes him too.

He knows that if the killer were to break in right now, he would be dead. Which is why he wants to let her know how he feels. She stands on the other side of the courtyard with her friends, where they all stand in a neat group and gossip. About him, in particular, because it's known that he likes her.

He tells himself that he will ask her today. That before the day is up, he will have tied up this one loose end.

There's this kid named Samantha. She likes Karl, knows that he likes her, and is watching him right now out of the corner of her eye. She can see him talking to some other girl and some other guy.

She stands with her friends. They all talk in hushed voices, some about the killer, but mostly about Karl. She smiles, liking being seen as an object of desire and the center of attention. She sees the clock, hanging on the side of the school building. There is a minute left until the day is over, until Karl leaves and she has to wait another twelve hours to see him again.

She curls her lip slightly, hating this feeling of waiting, but she keeps watching him. That's when she sees him break free of the other girl and start walking towards her. She brushes her hair back and puts on a winning smile, not noticing the look on the other girl's face, barely hearing the question he asks her, barely registering the words that come out of her mouth.

Yes.

There are these kids in a gym. They play ping pong with the threat of the killer hanging over them. It's Thursday: three days after the attacks, and they have heard that the police have surrounded the man on the motorcycle's house.

They stop their games for one moment, and the slap of balls against paddles stops. A teacher asks them to step outside. Karl and Samantha walk while holding hands. Beatrice walks far behind them.

She cried the last two nights. She cried because she saw them sitting together, because they held hands, because they didn't say anything to each other but seemed to love each other anyway. She cried because they were happy, and she wasn't, because everyone expected her to be happy for them, and she couldn't force herself to do that. She cried because she faked a stomachache to get away from watching her leaning into his shoulder, and because she hated lying.

She cries now too, silently, but not because of them. The teacher just asked them to hold a moment of silence for the people who were shot by the man on the motorcycle, who was under siege in his apartment three blocks from the school.

The minute lasts forever as the American students and the French students stand in a clump in the mud under a basketball hoop. Samantha scuffs the mud with her shoes and Karl lays a hand on her shoulder, silently signaling her to stop. Someone's timer goes off and the kids all exhale. They walk back to the gym, but Samantha stops, shakes Karl off, tells him, go without me.

Samantha's been thinking. She's watching everyone around Karl now, checking for any threats. She doesn't want to lose him after two days. She analyzes everyone he's been around, seeing if they could possibly take him away from her.

He hangs out with a lot of the guys: the two Jewish kids who hide in the bathroom because of the killer, the tall guy with the slowly growing moustache who hates everyone, the guy who talks about nothing but Skyrim. And the girl whom everyone thinks is a lesbian. But Samantha knows she's not, not after that time in fifth grade, when they used to be best friends, when the girl told her behind the playground that she really liked a new boy who talked too much.

Samantha sees how the girl hangs around Karl, how they get along so easily, how they can talk about anything. She sees how he smiles when she approaches, how she seems somehow prettier around him. And in that moment, Samantha couldn't care less about the killer and the minute of silence under the basketball hoop. She only knows that someone else likes Karl, and Samantha needs to get her away from him.

There's this kid in the courtyard, listening to the sirens blare outside the school. Beatrice strains her ears, she can just hear the shouts of police over the sound of rushing cars.

Belen Edwards, Grade 9
Washington International School / Writopia Lab
Washington, DC
Short Story, Gold Key

the cardinal and the blue jay
(excerpted)

Bale could taste snowflakes melting on his tongue as he walked, his damp boots leaving a trail of impressions in the milky blanket of snow. He brushed aside the branches of evergreens that smelled of pine needles and scoured the tree line for a promising trunk.

Dawn painted the dreary horizon with a faint orange tint, thawing the newly frozen lake and leaving fragments of mushy ice floating along the surface. The surrounding forest was utterly silent, as if it, too had been encased beneath the watery glass.

With a pat of his frosted glove, Bale made sure the hatchet still dangled from his belt as it tautly wrapped around his muscular frame. He reminded himself of his task: to chop down a pine for his village. The twigs would be whittled into utensils, or perhaps made into a broom, the bark used for a surface to scrawl writing on, the chunks of wood burned for fire, and the pine cones painted so that they could be hung as decorations. He smiled at the thought of their spiraling spikes and relaxing aroma.

At his remembrance of home and its comforts, fingers of cold crept through his ragged fur coat and chilled his spine. Shivers passed through his body, yet he trudged on with a serene pleasure.

His eyes alighted upon a pine that stuck out from the others, sprouting defiantly in the center of a bleak clearing by the water. Its thick trunk was a deep mahogany and entailed plenty of logs to keep his hut warm.

Bale began to head towards it, quickening his march, when he heard a peculiar chirp issue from the canopy above his head. He halted, and listened for a moment. It was a high pitched voice.

"A man disturbs our forest."

Bale looked around, but failed to see anyone among the brush.

Another voice that was slightly lower in pitch remarked, "Aye. Do you think he plans to take one of the trees?"

Again, Bale panned his stare across the wintry landscape, searching for the source, before finally noticing the silhouette of two birds on a branch in the canopy above his head. He spied the crimson frill of a male cardinal and its silver-tipped feathers. Beside it, a blue jay twitched its azure tufts dappled with white, which appeared as if the snow clung to them. The pinpricks of color gazed intently at each other through pupils lined with charcoal, despite their bodies' skittish movements along the limb.

Bale observed in awe as the cardinal's beak snapped open and closed.

"That's all they do it seems," muttered the rose bird.

He rubbed his eyes with disbelief as the blue jay desperately shrieked, "But our nests will be destroyed! Our eggs will freeze!"

Bale felt a pang of guilt, though he was not quite sure of its validity. He questioned whether his brain was deceiving him, only to be interrupted by another outburst.

The cardinal twitched its head, as if to shrug. "That is the way of life. We will move on and bring our offspring elsewhere."

The blue jay could not be quieted. "My babies are going to die! Can't we do anything?"

Bale fumbled to remove his woven wool cap as he strained his ears for the reply. He desperately wanted to hear the male's answer.

However, the velvet-cloaked cardinal only shrugged its wings again and shuffled its stick-like feet to the edge of the branch, as if to leave.

"Wait!" Bale called out. After the strangled cry escaped his mouth, he realized its childish tone. He had became a boy whining for his fantasies to stay.

The birds were startled and immediately fluttered away into the calm of the forest in a feathery cloud of pigment, leaving Bale to contort his moistened beard into a frown. He concentrated on the forest around him, attempting to eavesdrop on another conversation, but it appeared the spell had been broken. The only sound in the tranquil forest was the shallow dripping of snow melting.

Bale pondered a moment while flurries danced about him like silken butterflies He sighed, and resumed his trek towards the evergreen. A whisper of shame tugged at his heart as he noted that the trunk contained a cozy hollow, perfectly suitable as a residence for forest critters.

His hands fumbled with the strap on his belt as he unlatched the ax. He mentally cursed his cold fingers and the gloves that had failed to warm them.

When he had reached the pine, Bale reared up with the hatchet and gazed at the maroon trunk. The towering boughs were coated in snow, their network of branches laden with pine cones and needles. This was truly a healthy specimen. Then, with an apprehensive air, he began the chopping motion.

The glint of the ax blade sparkled in the early morning scene as it glided through the air. Suddenly,

Bale halted as he sensed the faint melody of a birdsong tickle his eardrums.

"There he goes."

A shrill outcry followed. "Please, no!"

In his hands, the metallic edge froze just as it made contact with the bark. Bale swiveled his focus through the sky and coppice, scouring for the source. A murmur issued from the branches in front of him, and with measured movements Bale maneuvered toward it.

As he freed himself from a sparse hedge, Bale was greeted by the sight of a nest, woven from sticks and caked in mud, balanced on a tree limb just above his head. In it, a quartet of miniature, cerulean eggs lay nestled in the speckled sapphire of a blue jay's plumage. He paused, realizing the utter innocence and beauty of the spectacle.

The navy bird glanced over Bale's body, shuffling nervously at the vision of his hatchet. Bale didn't comprehend at first, but quickly dropped the blade as he realized it was bothering the mother. "Sorry," he stuttered. In response, the bird calmed and peered at Bale through eyes that resembled the glistening pebbles of the stream bed.

"I express my gratitude to you, man from the village." With sharp twitches, the fowl gestured at herself and her eggs. "Your sacrifice is appreciated."

From high above in the web of wood, the burgundy of a cardinal fluttered down and alighted on the fringe of the nest. The male shook his feathered crown in agreement. "Perhaps I was wrong about you."

Bale regarded the pair of creatures with a dazed nod and smile, unsure of what to say.

"It was nothing." He turned around and began to leave, stumbling in the process.

"Thank you," the blue jay called over his shoulder.

A final remark from the cardinal rang out from behind him. "You forgot your ax!"

Bale continued to tread across the fluffy carpet. "I don't need it!" he hollered, and grinned as his taste buds felt the amused chill of a flurry on his tongue yet again.

Matthew Evenson, Grade 7
Rocky Hill Middle School
Clarksburg, MD
Science Fiction / Fantasy, Silver Key

she lit the sea

(excerpted)

To be polite, I will thank you for choosing this voice from the shelf that it had previously rested upon.

It was terribly cold on that shelf and extraordinarily lonely.

However, do take good care of me.

I'm fragile.

My pages are made from light whispers and I am bound by black sights.

I'm fragile.

Before we press on together,

A yield sign must escape from my pen.

The words you shall read are knives, and my tone flickers from black to light as if it were a dying bulb.

Beautifully, of course.

This tale will not be much of a roller coaster for you.

This is simply text.

It is as worthless as the drivel that assaults your diary.

I will never apologize for recording the truth.

Although, in truth, there have been times when I should have.

So, you'd better lawyer up, as there's no need for a soul in the oncoming dream.

No need at all.

* * *

I met my pen on the Eastern tides of the New World, in a shelter built by black gold.

Clouds would dance above the splashing waves, thickening the air with yet-to-have-fallen rain.

Three smiles beyond my holder's home wept a minor cliff, its connotation dangling by a thread.

When the car windows turned to fragile, cold glass is when I knew that I would meet my pen once more.

He would live his winter days in his cave with me, waiting for his mind to cooperate with what it used to be when light drowned the world.

She was a demon,

That darkness.

That cold.

A demon.

* * *

He would often envy the souls who floated beautifully to heaven,

And curse those who remained like him, trudging an ugly life on earth.

* * *

His genius jousted in chess each year.

In December, he would fight valiantly against Winter's pawns.

When the crisp leaves began to give up the warm hues and dance to the ground, he would know to gather his own pawns and join the dance.

Unfortunately, each year, when he grasped my life, I knew that he had lost to Winter.

He felt as though he should have been able to fight.

He drowned me when he thought about wanting to be smarter.

He wasn't smart enough.

* * *

I must have forgotten to mention,

The star of these words goes by Oliver.

I hope you love him as much as I do.

* * *

Oliver caught the knowledge of her like a miserable cold.

It was December, and his discovery had almost removed him from his bed-ridden state with illness.

Her voice seared his throat, her scent would clog his nose and her aura baked his skin to a crisp. In his mind, she was a boarder in his large, empty home. Through his bedroom window he would watch her linger in the surf. Her natural shoes involved themselves with the sea, kissing its love each morning.

Her hair entangled itself in the winter breeze and washed his face each morning.

* * *

Each morning, she would dance with Oliver's thoughts in the cold sand that he'd once loved and mock the waves of ice that could never reach their toes.

* * *

They danced.
And she would twirl.
And he would twirl.
And they would twirl.
They would twirl.

* * *

One morning, my words recall a *rap* at the front door. That patient *rap* jolted Oliver from his night to the door.

A rare endeavor.

"Is your mother home?" the voice of Oliver's neighbor floated on a rollercoaster before coming to a halt at the core of Oliver's mind.

"Who are you?"

My son spoke blatantly, nervous rudeness and fear dripping from his soured tongue.

I watched from my pages as her planetary eyes searched her mind for an answer.

"I'm Lucinda." She spoke carefully. "I prefer to be called Lucy, though."

Oliver wrung his hands.

"I'm Oliver." He spoke carefully. "I simply go by Oliver," he said.

He cursed the simplicity of his name.

He could only one day wish for a name that begged for a nickname.

Lucy's light in life blinded Oliver for the first of many times that morning.

* * *

Lucy invaded my home with a simple handshake.

This gesture Oliver was not used to.

"How lovely to meet you." Lucy smiled like a crescent moon. "Am I allowed in?"

Her question soared above Oliver's head.

"What?" he asked.

"Am I allowed to come into your home? You don't have to let me."

She stepped backwards from the door.

"No, no, come in."

Oliver gestured for the star to come down to his earth.

When Lucy entered the home, it was difficult even for me to ignore the light that followed her stride.

Oliver offered her a glass of light lemonade and sat across from her in the museum of a parlor that filled Oliver's home.

The seats cracked in agony when the pair sat and the dust of conversation fled when their backs settled into the room.

Oliver held me in my place beside him as he stared at Miss Lucinda.

I knew that Oliver knew that I knew that he was wondering if Lucy was wondering about him.

That moment was a riddle of moments.

* * *

I was left as an eye to watch Oliver speak with Lucy for hours.

They spoke of nothing relevant,

Yet,

To Oliver,

It felt as if they had spoken of everything.

He was so close to her,

Yet she seemed more mysterious than ever.

The pair floated in the air of his home for hours, dancing together in every word of nothing.

* * *

Oliver spent much time alone for the next few days.

He was still absorbing the glow from Lucy, in his room with no one but myself to witness.

* * *

He would have given anything to speak with Lucy again.

He would have given his wit.

* * *

If I turn back my own pages, I can recall a time when Lucy lit the day.

I slept in Oliver's lap as he scrawled his interior into my own.

He sat on his back porch, facing the beach.

Between strokes of his pen he would occasionally look up at the water.

It was rare for him to inhale fresh air, as he preferred his own air.

"Oliver?" He stopped my pen's work to look into the sun.

"Lucy!" His voice fattened with excitement.

Lucy trotted over from her home to where I sat and gently lifted me out of Oliver's lap.

I reveled in her grasp before she sat me on the floor.

"I haven't seen you."

She glowed.

Oliver cleared his throat.

"I tend to stay in my room."

He looked down.

Oliver could not stand to tell Lucy of his life.

He knew that his life, in comparison to Lucy's, was as if you were to compare an elegant chandelier to the small floor beneath.

"I've been thinking about you, you know," she said.

She looked into Oliver's hopelessly vacant eyes.

"I do know," Oliver choked, "I mean, I know *now*."

Lucy closed her mouth to smile.

"We should do something together, don't you think?" She offered.

Oliver stared at the floorboards beneath.

"No," he said.

Caroline Ewing, Grade 12
Edmund Burke School
Washington, DC
Short Story, Gold Key

the end of innocence

The house smells like burnt toast and Christmas trees.
My neck is wet from my dripping hair as I steal
downstairs to get paper for the wedding card for my old
babysitter I promised my mother I would make last
night.
I hold the paper casually by my neck to cover the
evidence, my battle scars.
Putting lights up on the tree, I brush by my dad and
choke on his smell—
I am transported to that night, in *his* car, me sitting like
on a bus seat, knees up on the seat in front of me.
That was not an invitation
For you to put your hands in my pants.
But you do
And I pull your head closer to mine like I enjoy it.
You never notice how many men there are in the world
until you wear a short skirt
You never notice how menacing the world is, how
much your life screams "Target! Target!" until you hear
about a gunman in an elementary school where they
thought they were just as safe as you feel now.
I am taken aback by how unprotected and bare I feel,
lying in the backseat of a harmless white Subaru, the
same one my parents had when I was little—the car
where when I fell asleep in the back I would wake up
the next morning in my bed.
I want to curl up on the seat and just have him drive me
home.
I go to the far side of the seat, to escape, breathing
room.
Oh no—he sees this as an offer

No no no
His buckle is undone
NO
I do it.
Abruptly, I sit up.
"Take me home."
His dazed face takes a while to register that
After empty inquiries as to whether or not I'm okay
(like he cares), he obliges.
Listlessly, I stare at the window
And pretend to care about what he's saying.
As we pull up to my house,
He leans over and kisses my cheek.
"I had a great time."
And all I can think about is the way he grabbed the
back of my head and yanked me towards him and
shoved his tongue into my mouth and I didn't even
want to do it and why is this happening to ME and this
is not what should happen on a first date and *why me?!*
That was my first date.
What a welcome to the world.
You never notice how profane your speech patterns are
until you are speaking with a friend in front of a five
year old.
You never realize how much you have grown, how
much innocence is gone until you look back.
And by then it is too late.

Kateri Gajadhar, Grade 10
Washington Lee High School
Arlington, VA
Poetry, Silver Key

little girls room

I spend my time at the mountain making
Faces. If I part my jaw just like this,
Tilt my head and press my tongue to the
Smooth of where teeth meet, I can
Almost remember what I am trying to catch.

And I used to make myself sad;
Trace the trees that treadmill past
School bus windows.
But it was decided
Sad was only beautiful with
Cigarettes and a gap through your thighs
Where you can fit four of your fingers
With knee-skulls locked.

I made those mouths and
Wasn't gracious.
I was boy with his first cigar/man at a
Brothel guilty
Machine hand kills the cat/chopsticks
To the brain guilty.

There were months of porcelain,
Of delicate boxes and pretty friends
Eating slices of Toast.
Then there was running the water
No One Will Hear and then
Buzzy eyes and falling. Even still

A patina of weakness clings
Soft on the hips.

Lara Haft, Grade 12
Richard Montgomery High School
Rockville, MD
Poetry, Gold Key and American Voices Nominee

restrictions

Katie runs past me as she cries out, "You'll love today's class, Daksha!"

I watch this American girl, her long, black hair flying behind her, free from any veil. Katie's my age, but her life is so different. She's still in school, with no child to take care of or husband to please.

She stands and talks to Chameli, her mother, our teacher, and my role model. Chameli has told us her story many times. How she escaped her abusive husband and hard life here to go to America, but now comes back to teach other women. "Empowering the women of India," she says.

Today, she asks us to volunteer and stand in front of the class. Talika steps forward and Chameli ties a long piece of black ribbon around Talika's ankles.

"Women in India must cover their ankles. This is one of your restrictions. I want you to tell me some more, and for each, I will tie a piece of this black cloth around Talika."

We are all silent for a while, not daring to speak so bluntly against those old traditions. Then a woman from the back says, "We are not allowed to speak for ourselves."

I look at the speaker. She is our oldest classmate.

Chameli wraps a ribbon around Talika's mouth. The silence has now been broken, and all the women are coming up with restrictions, shouting so that Chameli can hear us.

"We need to wear a veil."

A strip of cloth around her forehead.

"We must cover our shoulders."

A strip of cloth around her shoulders.

"We are not allowed to leave the house unless our husbands let us."

A strip of cloth around her feet.

"We cannot cook what we want."

A strip of cloth around her hand.

"We cannot wear what we want."

A strip of cloth around her waist.

"We cannot speak loudly."

A strip of cloth around her throat.

"We work all day, caring for our family, but cannot make decisions for ourselves."

A strip of cloth around her heart.

We can't stop.

Soon, Talika is almost completely covered in block cloth. We grow quiet as Chameli ties the last piece of fabric. I feel tears form as I think about my daughter, playing outside. She is innocent and free, but she will soon have to face the restrictions and unjust life of a woman. I promise myself that I will work hard to never let that happen. I will continue my education, I will help our village, and I will show that women are powerful and valuable. I won't be treated as weak and feeble anymore, and my daughter won't be either. I made this promise, and all around me, I knew the other women did as well.

Katarina Holtzapple, Grade 10
Washington Lee High School
Arlington, VA
Flash Fiction, Gold Key

looking out my cell window

Looking out my window, I see the sky
Envision me working on the cloud next to nine
Staring at the sun, I see to its core
The fire that burns around it is like a boy
A flame that is angry, pained and sad
Waiting to burn, since the day it was born

Looking out my window, I see the moon
Jumping on the stars, I am not that far
From the cool nice night that a boy wishes he had
He's bright like the moon, but small as Pluto
He runs through the night on a mission
He jumps over the broom, but is stuck with bad luck
Because he ran into a room, with no way out
Now the only thing he can do
Is watch the days and the nights fly past
Like a bird speeding past on a sunny day

Vision over
Lights out
Bedtime...

Malik Kettles, Grade 11
Free Mind Book Club and Writing Workshop
Washington, DC
Poetry, Silver Key

# of fire and fences
(excerpted)

Some sixth sense awakens me. I lay awake for a few seconds, my brain sluggishly rebooting from sleep. I become aware of sweat rolling off my body, and I kick the covers away. After a few seconds beneath the fan, I realize that I'm not getting any cooler. If anything, I'm feeling even hotter. How is that possible?

As I slide out of bed, I become aware of a faint sound. It's difficult to categorize, resembling something between a hiss and a crackle. I frown, searching my brain for anything I'd ever heard that resembled that noise. I come up blank.

And then my door flies open, and Papa stands silhouetted in the doorway. An unearthly light dances around his frame, and he yells something at me. I peer up at him, not comprehending. He runs up to me, grabs my shoulders, and shouts in my face.

"FIRE!" he yells.

Awareness floods through my body like electricity, and I'm jolted awake. My father pulls me up and we run down the hallway toward Milly's room. Her door is open, so I know she's already been awakened. Papa and I reach the stairs, and then I can see it for the first time: a hideous mixture of red, orange, and yellow, like the first three colors of the rainbow merged together or the spilled combination of a child's paint set. It creeps along with the leisurely pace of the invincible, and yet it also races. Toxic fumes resonate above the flames, clinging to the walls and ceiling. The noise grows to a dull roar, something akin to a crowd at a football game.

Papa and I hurry down the staircase. The inferno appears to be emitting from the kitchen, or perhaps the family room, so the stairs are clear at the moment. We bound to the bottom in seconds. Papa shoves me toward the front door, and I stumble.

"I'm going to find Milly and your mother!" he barks at me. "Stay outside, where it's safe!"

I turn back, but he's already dashing toward another room. My eyes start to burn. Acrid tears well up in their corners. I fumble for the doorknob as a fit of coughing assaults my lungs and ribs. The heat is intense. I can almost literally drink it like a liquid.

Mercifully, the knob twists open, and I gasp my way into the night air. It may be warm outside, but compared to the furnace inside, the night is a freezer.

I fall to my knees, greedily sucking in the fresh air. I look around at my surroundings. None of the other houses feature even a glimmer of light. Ours, on the other hand, looks like Los Angeles. But that's not what grabs my attention. What fixates me is Milly—or, rather, her absence.

Milly.

I look back at the house with apprehension. Mama's in there. Papa's in there. Milly's in there.

When I reenter the house, the sheer difference of it stops me. It barely resembles the home I knew. The fire dances elegantly along the floor, the walls, creating a nightmarish medley of light and shadow. The smoke lies like a heavy fog, making vision near impossible. I stagger my way along, managing to reach the living room without having to inhale. The smoke resides in this room, too, but it's not yet as thick, and though breathing is laborious, it's still possible.

"Milly?" I cry out. "Milly?"

"Milly!" another voice parrots, but it's Mama's voice. If I concentrate, I can discern her moving about in the other room. "Honey, where's Milly?" It sounds like Papa is with her.

"Milly!" he bellows, confirming my thoughts. "Don't worry, dear! We'll find her!" They found each other, at least.

If they don't have Milly, Milly isn't outside, and she isn't in her bedroom, then there's only one place she would have run to—the same place she flees to whenever our parents have a go at each other. Between the tears caused by the noxious fumes and the dense smoke, I can't see anything, but I know my house like I know Milly's screams of distress, and I blindly navigate my way to the dining room.

The smoke here is far thicker, and I double over in another fit of coughing. My eyes feel like they're gushing rivers of lava. I feel my way over to one of the chairs and whip it away from the table.

"Milly!" I call at the table. "Milly!"

Faintly, like a whisper on the wind, barely audible over the roaring flames, comes her reply.

"Tu-tu!" Her voice, filled with horror, drives into me like a sword.

"Milly! Milly!" I call for her mindlessly, over and over, operating on instinct. I see a flash of movement, and Milly crawls out from beneath the table.

"Tu-tu!" she wails, seconds before I lift her into my arms. I tuck her in close to my chest. Holding her securely, I bolt toward the front door, but the sight of flames arrests my progress. The blaze, having reached the entryway, mocks me as it prevents our escape, promising to make our house our tomb.

"STUART!" a voice roars, and I turn to see Papa, ashen, sweating, coughing, but alive, Mama tucked against his side. He motions for me to follow. I do.

Papa leads us to the back door. The fire continues to spew fumes at us, like the exhaust from an antique car, only far more lethal. We're all coughing and hacking now. Mama struggles with the sliding glass door, which seems determined to open as slowly as possible.

"Open!" Mama shrieks, tugging at the door. Papa helps her, and together, they force it open. We spill out into the backyard as the flames fill the doorway behind us. They snarl, as though alive, filling our home with heat and light and noise. The sound now reminds me of something: the Rice Krispies breakfast this morning—snaps, crackles, and pops. But this is coupled with a roar.

Mama's banging on the fence, apparently trying to knock it down, but that's no good. I remember how much effort Papa put into building this fence. Impenetrable, that's how he described it. Animalistic fear fills Papa's face as he realizes that we're trapped, and he too begins pounding on his creation. Together, they pound and hammer at the fence.

Ben Koses, Grade 12
West Springfield High School
Springfield, VA
Short Story, Honorable Mention

dooda alah (no friend)
(excerpted)

They picked up each ring with gentle fingers. He couldn't help but wonder what the couple was thinking. Now, they weren't wedding bands, but their eyes were glued to the rings. He'd known Alex since he was born. He'd watched him grow up and remembered him running through his store, almost tipping over the balanced shelves and each time catching them just before they fell. He'd watched him find sticks in the dirt and draw airplanes and rockets, things he had only seen from afar. Now the shopkeeper stayed silent, listening to the murmurs of the two apparent lovers, their fingers intertwined.

"This one's beautiful. It goes with your eyes," Alex said.

The shopkeeper cringed at the exchange of loving words between a Diné man and a white woman, they disgusted him. He continued to watch, keeping a close eye on them as they wandered through the store exploring the other jewelry.

Whites are capable of corruption and the destruction of entire communities, he thought. His mind wandered, reluctantly, to his own childhood. He thought of the white park rangers who drove onto the reservation to take the children away. Everyone knew when they were coming long before they arrived because the sound of the engine was the white people and the sound of hooves on dense sand were Diné. You could trust the hooves, but not the engines. As soon as they were able to make out the sounds in the distance, his family was set into action. They hid in twos, one brother with each sister. They ran as fast as they could to the protruding rocks, where there were crevices and caves. They were to climb as high as possible on the rocks and hide out of sight until their father came to get them. The sound of one heavy-chested breath could carry across the silent reservation. They would not risk saying a word. He and his sister would cuddle in the cave of the rock, a cave that they might otherwise be playing in, and wait until their father appeared around the corner. That was the best moment of his life: each time his father appeared around the corner. Until one day he didn't appear.

Quickly shaking away the thought of that day, he walked across the shop floor and over to the couple. "Alex," he said.

"Bidziil, these rings are beautiful. Who made them?" "I did, thank you." And although he knew very well the answer to the question, he asked, "Who is this woman you are with?"

Alex smiled and replied, "This is Jane, my fiancé." To Jane, "That is the word, right?" She nodded.

"Oh, congratulations," Bidziil replied reluctantly, but he was not surprised. There were rumors going around the reservation. "I will be closing up in a few minutes," he said.

"Okay, we were just leaving."

* * *

Bidziil's mind fell back to that moment. The moment they arrived at their hogan at dusk and their father was in it, covered in his own blood, lying in their mother's lap. They had waited until the sun began to set for him to come and find them. But he never came. So they took the chance and returned home. They knew they were not supposed to be outside of the hogan in the dark. It was instinct to return home. Maybe, he thought, their *azhé'é*, father, could not find them or climb the tall wall anymore, he was growing old, or maybe their *amá*, mother, had taken ill and he had stayed home to take care of her. The answer was clear once they arrived at the hogan. Their mother told them that their brother had taken their sister to collect herbs and flowers. Their job was to use wet rags to clean his wounds.

It was an unsaid understanding. Whites had done this to their father and they would be back. Sooner than usual.

* * *

"*Yá'át'ééh*! Welcome!" Alex's mother, Haseya, was trying to better her English, so she had started saying everything twice. It helped Jane learn the Navajo language. She would repeat the words back to herself in her head and occasionally, when she was by herself, she would say them out loud. Living on the reservation was an adjustment for Jane. In the year that she'd been going back and forth between her house in Flagstaff and the rez, she had already learned all of the uses for the many parts of the buffalo—though they rarely ever saw buffalo—and how to bless and slaughter a goat, which became one of her regular tasks. The reservation astonished her. It was a self-sustaining community, not only physically, but emotionally. Members of the clans were so close they called each other brother and sister even if they hadn't met each other before. Jane didn't know, in going there to teach, that she would actually be the one learning the most.

The school she taught at was right outside the reservation and while many of the children on the rez were raised traditionally, some of them attended the school. She taught these kids but sometimes adults as well. She focused on those that, because of language barriers or other reasons, needed more help than was provided in the classroom. This often placed the children from the rez in her classes. They taught her a great deal about their culture through the stories they wrote. She learned Navajo words. It fascinated her, the amount of knowledge they stored in their heads without recognition. They were taught as young children how to cultivate the peach trees that were their families livelihood. At age eight they could support their family and then many were sent to European-American school to learn how to survive in the settler society. That didn't come as naturally to many of them.

Alex had gone to European-American school. He'd never liked it as much as the stories and instructions his mother would give him as they prepared the freshly slaughtered mutton for dinner. His mother was his idol at times. As a leader of the tribe, she had influence that he could only imagine. But she only used her influence when necessary. She was the most accepting person he knew.

Alex could hardly remember his father being around as a child. He would occasionally stop by but his mother never let his father stay long. The only memories he had of his father were coated with the stench of alcohol. Maybe once every couple of months his father would come over to their hogan. Each time it was the same routine. He would stumble over to Alex and tell him he missed him very much and that he was working hard to make money for him and his mother. Then he would make his way to Haseya and attempt to kiss her lips but every time she turned her head and his lips only managed to find her cheek. This would make him mad for a moment but he would quickly forget where his anger stemmed and return to his original goal: money. The only point of these visits was for his father to gain a little bit more money for booze.

When he was young, Alex loved these visits. He believed the lies his father fed him. But as he grew older the visits only made him hate his father. With each visit Alex hated his father more and more. With a drunk for a dad, his mother raised him on her own. She'd lived through assimilation and was taken away to boarding school when she was eight, yet she almost always had a smile on her face.

Once when he'd asked her how she did it she replied, "Because I have my *ashkii*, my son."

He smiled and didn't question it further.

Genevieve Kules, Grade 11
Duke Ellington School of the Arts
Washington, DC
Short Story, Silver Key

the elevator

Ground Floor of Wilson High School

The number of us who ride the elevator is always changing. 5+1+2-2+3-3+6-4+2-5. There are only five of us who remain throughout the year. Two of us in wheelchairs, one of us blind, one of us with a full-time nurse, and me. I get on the elevator, get off, go to class. The steps of my shoes are imprinted on the floor, the constant pressure, year round, wearing the ground away. Maybe, if I ever come back after I graduate, I will still be able to see where I stood. My corner.

Hold Doors

Every few days there is one person who asks me why I am on the elevator. Sometimes a teacher, sometimes a school administrator. I make it a game of how I answer, each time different. "None of your business." "Blood pressure disorder." A stare. "Postural Orthostatic Tachycardia Syndrome, POTS for short. Every time I stand up, my body doesn't maintain homeostasis, and I get really dizzy and sick, and-" they usually cut me off by then. Because, none of them *really* want to know why I'm on the elevator. They just want to question. It's not every day that you see someone that's sick, but doesn't look sick at all.

Maximum Occupancy

I get to know all of us.

Adam, in the wheelchair, the one who waves and smiles, even on Mondays. His aide feeds him his lunch.

Amy, who broke her leg playing soccer.

Nicole, whose eyes are the biggest I've ever seen, whose heart sometimes skips beats. Her nurse wears scrubs with Disney characters on them, different for each day of the week.

Minus Amy.

Dan, who is on crutches for three weeks after twisting his ankle, skiing.

Liz, who is blind, asked me to walk her to the bus. She links her arm in mine. I describe everything around us, the stairs, the door, the metal detectors, the students. I wanted her to see. She looks at me, at where my voice is coming from. I wonder if all she sees is dark. I wonder if the colors that we see are the words that she hears.

Minus Dan.

Katie, whose toe got skated over at the rink.

Nora, who always rests her head on her shoulder. It never moves, just stays tilted to the side. Her aide makes her laugh while she pushes her around in the wheelchair.

Minus Katie.

And so it goes.

In Between Floors

We are all different, but we are all the same. Us five. I don't see them very often. Long periods of time elapse when they are gone and I am here, alone on the elevator with the others. I hate it. Because they are the only ones to understand what it is like to be sick every day. There's no cast that will help us heal, no crutches that will carry us through our lives. When we are on the elevator, we look at each other, smile our smile.

We do not ask, we do not question.

Going Up

I start to feel better at the beginning of the year. Each step is lighter, my backpack is not as heavy, my head does not press down on my neck. The elevator key, though, is heavier in my pocket. The doctors say that my blood pressure disorder is getting better. They thought it would get better, but not so quickly. My body is fighting back. I am fighting back. I am the highest functioning patient they know of. It is not because the syndrome is not as bad. It's because I am fighting as hard as I know how. What they don't know is that I'm fighting for all of us.

Call For Help

My friend asks me to walk down one flight of stairs with her. It is during lunch. Everyone is outside. It is not crowded, so I will not be pushed. I nod my head. She would try to catch me if I fall. She couldn't, though. I walk down the stairs. I have not done it in over a year. My legs shake, and I hold the handrail. I wonder if this is how a baby feels when it walks for the first time.

For a moment, I close my eyes, and I am surrounded by students: pushing, shoving, yelling. I am in ninth grade, my body is small, hunched over. My lungs constrict, I try to breathe, but I am falling down the stairs, like in a dream, my arms extended.

I open my eyes. I am still standing. I have walked down the stairs. My friend smiles at me.

I don't cry. But almost.

Out of Service

My steps are the steps that they will never take, the steps they take but will never see, the steps they will never be able to take alone.

Emergency Stop

When I go to visit colleges in the spring, I take the tours with my parents. Overall, looking at seven different campuses, over thirty thousand people, I see only one girl in a wheelchair. There are handicapped entrances and exits, handicapped ramps, handicapped elevators…but no handicapped. I tell that to my mother. "Lillie, you won't need to use the elevator in college. You'll be better by then." That is not the point. It is that when I am gone, Adam, Nicole, Liz, and Nora will all still be there on that elevator. One day at a time, one class at a time. They are stuck, stuck in their bodies, stuck in the dark, stuck in wheelchairs, stuck in doctor offices and waiting rooms. Stuck because of nothing that they could control. So how is it that I am the one who now gets to walk up the stairs?

Call Cancellation

On the first day of school after Spring Break, when Adam waves and smiles at me, I can barely smile back. His aide is telling him some story, and he is laughing, and I am thinking that his laugh is more genuine than any other I have heard before, and how he has a much harder life than almost all of us, but is somehow still happier. Just for a moment, I forget where I am. I forget the loud, cramped hallways, I forget the people pushing and shouting and yelling. I smile.

Going Down

I wonder if I come back if they will still be there. They will not graduate in four years. 1+1+1+1, the time grows longer and longer, and my time here grows shorter and shorter. But they will still be here.

Floor 4: Adam

I will always appreciate being able to feel the ground under my feet.

Floor 3: Liz

I will never take for granted being able to watch the sun rise and set, and rise again.

Floor 2: Nora

I won't always be kind, or say the right things. But I will always love that I have the opportunity to speak.

Floor 1: Us

I will always be included in us. I have never been anywhere where I was so accepted. We understood each other. We were not just the sick students. We were the elevator riders. And they knew that I was different than they were. That I would get out. That I would get better. But they didn't care.

Ground Floor

I sometimes wonder if Liz would rather go to a school for the blind, if Nora and Adam would rather go to a school where they weren't the only ones in wheelchairs and having their aides feed them their lunch. Because then they wouldn't have to worry if they were only unique because they were handicapped. Then, they would see what I see. They would see Nora, in her wheelchair in the corner of our school's atrium, everyone else running and laughing. They would see Adam, grinning at his friends while his aid spoon-feeds him applesauce. They would see Liz, navigating hallways full of people, only with a white cane to feel her way. They would see the four bravest, strongest people I have or will ever know. Even if they will spend their lives on elevators.

Doors Opening

I wouldn't blame them if they were angry. I would be. Why them, and not someone else? Why were they the ones that had to be so sick? But, as I have learned, it is too hard to continue to question. It takes too much energy, wondering why. Because, at some point, you have to accept it. The guilt and relief of getting better, the knowledge that you will be free from the elevator. But despite all that, you have to decide where you're going. There's no left or right, diagonal or zigzag. There are only two directions. You're either going down, or you're going up.

Lillie Lainoff, Grade 12
Woodrow Wilson High School / Writopia Lab
Washington, DC
Personal Essay, Gold Key and American Voices Nominee

there once was a man

There once was a man. Every day at precisely eight, his wife left for work, if she was not on a business trip. Half an hour later, he took his daughter to school and then went off to his work, wearing a crumpled dress shirt and tie. He worked for eight hours, sitting in front of a computer screen in a generic cubicle. He left at exactly five each day, picked up his daughter at Extended Day, and arrived home between 5:30 and 5:35. He made dinner and ate with his daughter at 6:30. When she was in town, his wife arrived home at seven and ate whatever was left. He put his daughter to bed at 8:30, and went to bed himself an hour later, after watching some TV. His wife came to bed some time later.

There once was a chubby, ugly man. He had a useless job, and stubbornly held on to it to "support me," as if I needed it. As a business executive, I had to spend a lot of time on business trips, but I made more than enough money. Plus, those business trips were a good way for some...extracurriculars. Regardless, the man was a burden, but his daughter was sweet, and he was nice in his own ways.

There once was an awesome daddy. He always did nice things for me. He always brought me to school. He gave me lots of gifts, too. Usually, after school he helped me with schoolwork, even though he wasn't very good at helping with writing, just math. He never got mad like mommy does when she helps. He always smiled when he saw me, and then hugged me. He was a great daddy.

There once was a dull man. He had been with the firm for years, but he never managed a meaningful promotion. Of course, he never got into any trouble either. He just did his job, then went home. He had very few friends in the office, and never came to any work events. It seemed to me he lived only for his daughter, and maybe his wife.

There once was a rather sad man. Sometimes I think I was his only friend, if you could even describe me as a friend. I would sit with him at lunch during work, although he didn't talk too much. I could occasionally get him to talk sports for a bit, but never for long. The only thing he would ever talk about for very long was his daughter, but even then, he seemed far away. He might have been depressed, but I don't think so. He just never seemed all the way there.

There once was a changed man. His wife was never around, and he never seemed to talk to anyone in the neighborhood. He used to be different. Not many people remember, but he used to come to parties, and greet people quite cheerfully. I think his head was messed up in that accident he had a few years ago, but nobody likes to talk about that.

There once was a good nephew. He had done well with himself wife-wise, and his daughter was beautiful. He even spent a sizeable chunk of his time helping his parents out as they got old. Then, they died in that nasty accident. I think he felt guilty, even though he wasn't driving. He just wasn't the same after that.

There once was a predictable man. He left the house at the same time every day, like clockwork. One morning, knowing he wouldn't be back for hours, I broke into his house, and started rummaging through his stuff, looking for valuables. Unfortunately, on that day, the man had forgotten something. I had my back to the door when he opened it. He shouted something, and I turned. He swung his briefcase at me, so I ducked, pulled out my gun and shot twice. The man stood motionless for a second, then raised the suitcase again. I don't remember anything after that.

There once was a frightened man. He had just walked in on, and somehow incapacitated, an armed burglar. He seemed to quake as he talked to me, and even twitched a little. He wouldn't even unbutton his suit coat for the paramedic. His case seemed like a relatively generic one, but a few things didn't add up. Neighbors reported gunshots, and the burglar's gun was missing a couple of rounds, but the bullets were nowhere to be found, and they clearly had not hit the man.

There once was an unhealthy, possibly traumatized man. He had just been robbed, but that didn't seem to be his only problem. He was somewhat overweight, and had a nervous twitch. He refused to let me examine him, except verbally. He also appeared to have some underlying personality disorder, although it may have just been the stress of being robbed.

There was once an odd man. He came to my hardware store in the middle of the afternoon, visibly twitching, and smelling like smoke. He bought an odd assortment of mechanical parts, then left, putting down the exact change on the counter without a word. I watched him go in wonder.

There once was a very strange man. He was compelled by the police to come in for a general checkup and psychiatric evaluation. He had just been robbed, and an on-site paramedic reported odd behavior after examining him. When I did the checkup, the man no longer had the nervous twitch the paramedic reported, but there were other odd things.

While he was fat, he did not look like he weighed five hundred pounds, which is what the scale reported. Additionally, his skin was incredibly smooth, and alternated hot and cool patches. I couldn't find anything else wrong with him though, so I reluctantly released him to the psychiatrist. After that, I never saw him again.

There once was an un-diagnosable man. He was referred for my evaluation by the police. At first I thought he was simply depressed, but he never showed any real signs, except a strong antisocial tendency. I quickly learned that he was happy, but quiet. Yet there was something unavoidably strange about him. He clearly had some sort of personality disorder, but it was like nothing in the books. I eventually just gave up trying to diagnose him, made my report, and released him back home.

There once was something very strange. It looked human, and it acted mostly human. It had lived as a man for years, and never had any reason to be suspected, until it was robbed and examined by a doctor and a psychiatrist. It did not seem particularly surprised when I burst into its house and apprehended it. I wanted it destroyed, but my superiors heard none of it, and it was soon whisked off to some government lab.

There is a robotic man. It has the brain of a human, but the body of a robot. I don't know who made it, or why, but it is an amazing case study. Perhaps we could find a way to weaponize it, but we'll need funding. Meanwhile, I'll have to write a letter to its family informing them that it died in "an accident."

There was once a man. He died in a car accident, in such a way that his spine was crushed, but his brain stayed alive. I took his brain, hid what was left of the body, and performed my experiment. Part of his brain had lost oxygen, but he lived. He lived.

David Lanman, Grade 10
Thomas Jefferson High School
Alexandria, VA
Science Fiction / Fantasy, Gold Key

safety

Sitting facing the glassy lake in silence, I adjusted my eleven-year-old legs, leaning as far to my left as I could. Dad, on my right, clasped his hands in his lap. We both waited that night on the floating dock, hoping that the other would begin the conversation. The water lapped onto the dark wood when the wind blew and we both curled a little deeper into our coats. The silence bellowed between us. I needed to tell him. I was the only one to protect Hope, but I could not release the words. They were dwelling in my throat, begging me not to speak them. But he needed to know. Looking down at my feet, fiddling with my hands as I sat on the wooden bench, I began talking, slowly and quietly, so he had to lean in to hear me:

"This is really hard to say. I need you to listen, okay? Hope and I love you and we would never want to hurt you but we don't want to come to your house anymore on the weekends. Would it be okay with you, please, if we only come on Wednesdays?"

There. I had finally gotten that part out of myself, where it had been gnawing for weeks, and into the open. At last, he knew what we wanted, maybe even understood.

He shot back, "Why? You've always liked it there."

"Dad, we just don't feel comfortable there. That's all." I tried to speak in my oldest voice, but I still couldn't look at him.

"Why?"

I couldn't say it. It would cut through him, hurting him too much. But if I didn't say anything we would have to go back. I would be forcing Hope to spend more nights there. I was the only one who knew what it was really like with him. I needed him to understand.

"We don't always feel safe."

"Safe? I've never hurt you. How could you feel unsafe?"

"Well, you drive a little too fast."

"No I do not. I drive just fine. Have we gotten in an accident? Have I gotten pulled over? No."

"But it feels really fast. And I can see the speed from the passenger's seat."

"You're seeing it wrong."

I breathed slowly and stared at my feet, forcing myself to get the next words out, the words he needed to hear:

"There is some more. You're not always around. I mean, you leave for hours and we don't know where you go."

"I am getting groceries for you. And working. I'm never gone for longer than I should be."

"I'm only eleven and Hope's only five and Mom says you're not supposed to leave us alone because we're too little. She says it's illegal. Last time you were gone, Hopesie fell."

"Hope was fine when I got back."

"When you're home you lock yourself in your room."

"I'm working. You expect me not to do my job?"

I needed to say the final piece; he wouldn't listen otherwise. I raised my head and continued in a whisper: "You get angry. You yell. Sometimes you even get really close and scream at us."

"I don't know what you're talking about. I never yell at you. A father should never yell at his daughter. I can't believe you think I do that."

"But it's true."

Dad bolted up and turned towards me, clenching his fists. He stood above me, glaring down with narrowed eyes from nearly six feet up, his broad chest and huge stomach leaning over me. I bent backward away from him. My knees came into my chest and I folded my middle to become as small as I could.

"Ellie, I would never hurt you. How can you even think that?" he yelled from above.

"I never said you hurt us. I just said that I get afraid. And I can't always get in front of Hope when you get angry. Or calm her down afterward. And then you leave."

"And where do you think I am? I make food for you. I bring you to your mom's house when you want. I pay for your fucking school."

"I know. Thank you."

"And what? You tell me you want to spend even less time with me?"

I couldn't answer. How could I abandon him like that? But, no, I couldn't spend another weekend with him, with Hope curled up with me in my bed every night. I stood up slowly and turned toward the plank walk that headed home.

He grabbed me before I could take a step, gripping my upper arms and turning me hard. He pushed me, holding his arms straight out, and I stumbled backward toward the edge of the dock. His eyes flew open and he began shaking me with every word:

"I am your father. I deserve to see you more than I do. I only see you half the time now and you want to cut that even more?"

He tilted me backwards. I could see the cold, wavy water under me. His hands tightened with each syllable. I tried to push forward but he held me on the edge of the wood. There was no reason to scream; no one would have heard me. Home was a full five minutes away, running.

Just as he leaned me back, another softer voice began whispering authoritatively from behind him, its identity hidden by his broad shoulders. "Johnny, put her down."

Following the voice instinctively, he released his hands and moved to the side, allowing her to step in front of me. I rushed forward, leaping into Grandma's arms, thanking her for stopping him. She hugged me deeply and patted my hair, trying to stop me from hyperventilating:

"Johnny, really, you should not have grabbed her like that. Look at her arms. She has welts. Ellie, tell me what's wrong."

"I love him, Grandma. He's my dad. I was just telling him that I would rather be home with Mom on the weekends. That's all. I would still see him on Wednesdays."

"With your mother? So has your dad not done enough for you? Hasn't he brought you to your soccer games?"

"No, he has."

"Has he not made you dinner? And watched the TV shows you like?"

"No, I mean, he has done all of that." I nodded.

She continued, patting my hand a little too hard, "So why would you want to desert him like that?"

I stammered, "I would never want to hurt him. It isn't about deserting him. I just would rather be home."

She stepped forward, still holding my hand but forcing me to retreat back towards the edge.

"Home? With your mother? The same mother who took you away from your loving dad?"

"She didn't take me away. The court gave her custody."

With nearly as much force as her son had bellowed, she said, "Your mother? She won't be with you. She's too focused on herself. On her career. She doesn't care for you or your sister. But your father. He plans his trips out of town around his time with you. He works to pay for your school and your life."

Dad stepped next to his mother, towering over me again as she continued, clutching my hand and not letting go. "Children must respect their fathers. Your dad does everything for you and you desert him and run to your narcissistic writer of a mother. You father has given everything to you, and you don't appreciate him. You are my granddaughter, and I expect you to honor your family and teach your sister respect."

I pushed between them, pulling back my hand and freeing myself. I began running toward home. Trying to get to Mom before Dad could catch me. Trying to reach Hope before they convinced me to stay.

Elizabeth Lasater-Guttmann, Grade 12
Georgetown Day School
Washington, DC
Personal Essay, Gold Key

survival

I watched as the crop of silver that topped my grandfather's head weaved in the crowd. I tried to keep up. The cracked asphalt was still wet from the drizzle earlier that day, but that hadn't put a damper on the peoples' spirit. Plastic tarps and slipshod wooden tables crowded the streets. Laid out was a myriad of produce. Tables strained under the weight of four-foot long winter melons. Tubs of submerged tofu with water as yellow as the bean curd lined the stalls. Caged geese and chickens competed against each other to be the most obnoxious as their squawks filled the narrow alley. Vendors shouted over the cacophony of animal, motor, and human noise. Even louder were the customers haggling with the sellers for a bargain. Two stalls over, hands waved frantically as they explained how they could get beef for half the price. A flash of silver in the corner of my eye told me to focus. I threaded my way through with only a fraction of my grandfather's grace, bumping into people and muttering apologies as I went.

At last I caught up with my grandfather as he sipped tea from a stained porcelain cup. Perched upon his cracked plastic chair, YeYe looked for all the world like he'd been relaxing there for hours. He was almost eighty years old, and decades of smoking had taken its toll on his lungs, but his long, confident strides had put him far ahead of me. I sat down next to him and tried to take it all in.

Somehow, in the heart of Nanchang, amidst the modernity of towering skyscrapers and gleaming cars, I found myself at a farmers market, Nongmao Shichang.

Looking down, the ground was rife with potholes and dirty brown water leaking into the streets from uncontrolled sewage. Mottled brick walls rose up on either side of the street as a constant reminder that we were still in the city, but the squawks of animals and the din of the people rose as a defiant and incongruent cry. This abandoned section of the city had found new life. Life that, to this 15-year-old, was too disorganized, too loud, and too dirty.

I asked my grandfather why there were so many people here. Why couldn't they be normal and buy food from a grocery store? Why didn't they get real jobs? YeYe gave a raspy chuckle as he did whenever I said something that betrayed my age. He told me to look around, to which I indignantly responded that I already had. He shook his head at my jejune attempts to understand his words. I stood up and craned my neck, trying to catch any detail that I'd missed. The raucous ambience was starting to get to me. My eyes stung from the smoke and dust that replaced oxygen in the narrow alleys of the farmer's market. I sat back down, angry at myself for not having an answer to my grandfather's impossible riddle. Grandfather took a long slurp of tea, set the cup down and folded his hands across his stomach. The answer he gave was so simple that I instantly felt foolish for not thinking it.

"Look at the people," he said.

My tunnel vision cleared like thick smoke blown away by the fresh breeze of my grandfather's words. A loud shout drew my attention to a man three stalls down. He was a butcher from the looks of the bloodied apron that clung tightly to his stout frame and the dull cleaver he raised in the air. The tendons in his arm were as thick as the meat he chopped. Each powerful blow cleaved the meat in two, which he then hung on the hooks above his stall. Black flies danced around his head and on the meat, but he would not be distracted. He turned and hoisted up another slab of meat. This was a man who excelled at his craft.

A loud banging sound made me spin around. Behind us a woman furiously beat a fish against a wooden board. Her weathered, wrinkled skin told me she was about the same age as my grandmother. Grime coated her face, and when she opened her mouth to speak to a customer, I noticed numerous dark gaps where teeth once were. She squatted on a tiny stool no more than a foot off the ground. Her back was bent at a painful angle over the small tub of live fish that swam in front of her. With speed that betrayed her age, she grabbed a waggling silver sliver out of the tub. The fish glistened even in the dim light of the narrow alley and must have been extremely slimy, but her grip was firm. She dashed the fish vigorously against a wooden board, stunning it. Grabbing a pair of scissors from behind her, she cleaned the fish and bagged it.

My eyes roamed the streets. Produce stalls lined the alley, but I'd seen more than enough. The sight of something familiar caught my attention. The movie *Inception* along with hundreds of American and Chinese movies alike covered a table. Some movies were old classics, but some were so new they were still in theatres. I had stumbled upon a stall that sold pirated DVDs. A young boy, no more than eight, sat and watched Chinese cartoons on a tiny television. An older vendor just past college age watched over the boy and kept an eye on the DVD display. His glasses were dirty, and the left lens was cracked, but that didn't seem to bother him. He thumbed through the assortment of DVDs, organizing them as he did, much like a librarian.

My grandfather cleared his throat, signaling it was time to go, so I stopped watching.

YeYe expectantly asked me what I'd observed. I told him in my broken Chinese what I had witnessed. He nodded while I talked. The butcher stayed at the farmer's market because he knew nothing else. As China industrialized, the world needed less manual labor and skill. Machines could cut meat twice as effectively without human error. The old woman with the fish most likely had been left behind as the world changed. She had nothing left but her hand-to-eye quickness. As time progressed, those who went with the flow and left the fields eventually ended up in the bright streets of Nanchang, and those who survived ended up in the narrow streets of Nongmao Shichang. She, along with most of the elderly vendors there, had not let go of the old ways.

YeYe told me the biggest tragedy and the biggest hope was in the DVD vendors. They were the ones born into poverty, and they would not escape it, at least not in their generation. The young man, Grandfather told me, most likely took the Gao Kao, the Chinese college entry exam, and had not done well. This would most likely mean a life of poverty, and the greatest tragedy was that many of the skills he'd learned in school would never be applied again. The hope of the family now lay in the younger child. I secretly hoped he'd succeed, but my grandfather said the environment of Nongmao Shichang is not conducive to learning.

The heat of the alley had begun to die down by now. It was far past noon, and I realized we had spent almost an hour just sitting and observing. It was then that we realized we had forgotten the first reason why we came to the farmer's market—to buy groceries. YeYe, with his powerful strides and knowledge of the streets, quickly finished the shopping. Before we left, we passed by the DVD vendor stall again. Only two DVDs had been sold and the rest untouched. I couldn't help but look once again at the younger boy and his brother, and a pang of sadness shot through my heart. My grandfather saw the look on my face and understood. As we left the twisting alleys of Nongmao Shichang, he told me the most important words I'll ever hear in my life. "Not all people are as fortunate as you have been."

William Liu, Grade 10
Thomas Jefferson High School
Alexandria, VA
Personal Essay, Gold Key

the umbrella parade
(excerpted)

And her name is Soar. And this is the day of the Umbrella Parade. The gigantic festival every girl waits for. When you are a girl at the Umbrella Parade, it is said that you will meet the love of your life under one condition: you catch the single, colorful, Chinese umbrella they throw off the highest building of the town. Last year, Soar caught it. And now comes her death. The girl who is married to death. That is Soar.

She stood at the top of her apartment building, which had not yet been demolished by incoming bombs. She scanned the bleak, war torn city around her and cursed to herself.

She screamed out angrily to the smoke covered sky, only adding to the insanity of the atmosphere. Soar clutched her head at the jumble and at the confusion and at the uncertainty of her life. It had begun only days before, but had seemed like an eternity since her head had stood still. She was becoming mad, and living off adrenaline, for a girl who is married to death can never know love. Below her, the bakery at the end of the street had set on fire and the screams of its inhabitants joined the continuous wail of the city. Soar shook her head and imagined a regular parade day.

She would wake up and sit under the hot water of the shower, and wash herself so cleanly that she would sparkle and glisten whenever she moved. She would carefully apply her makeup and shape her eyes into perfect little ovals, and make her face seem flawless and round. She would have a servant bring her the year's dress, which would fit her perfectly.

She would walk into the streets and all the other girls would look at her in silence, jealous and mad that they could not be so pretty and wonderful. She thought about this to calm her head. She had done it all this morning. Best to look good on the day of your end. Best to uphold tradition. Best to keep telling yourself everything is all right.

Soar looked back into the absolute destruction before her and set her now messy brows. She combed them back into place with her fingers and listened. Car alarms, babies, people, fire department sirens, police horns all telling people to get to cover.

A scream ripped open the close air and smashed right into the apartment's foundation. The structure shuddered and began to slowly spill into the street. Soar screamed and picked up her dress. As the apartment passed the building next to hers, she jumped, letting her 2,000-dollar heels fall into the stew below. Her arms caught a hanging gutter, and Soar struggled to pull herself onto the roof. She made it onto the safety of the cement and watched as her home crumbled on top of itself.

Soar made herself move again as she turned onto the horizon. She remembered why she came up to the rooftops in the first place. To find the plane. It had started with only rumors, but they had soon come true, when people heard a small plane pass over their homes at night. One old lady named Matilda said that they had planes like that when she was a young girl, around 2010. Soar looked down into the city below and spotted it. It was about a mile away, on the very edge of the city, where the suburbs and space center met. She could get there in eight minutes if she tried. Soar found a fire escape on the north edge of the building and swept down the ladders, all the while cursing to herself as her dress ripped and her makeup smeared. She looked for the plane again, and found it, people shoving and rioting to try to secure a seat on the plane. She cursed again and her mind began to shut, at the thought of being left there, with no one to save her. Being alone in a scary and dying city. Soar crazily ripped her hair out of its bun and tore off the rest of her dress, stripping down to her underwear. She jumped inside the next apartment and grabbed the first good pair of shoes she could find. She looked at them for a second as they were last season's Kinet. Soar slapped herself and shoved the shoes onto her feet, squeezing her toes.

Soar scrambled her way down the stairs and jumped to the street. More bomb sirens went off and Soar ducked behind some rubble to avoid being seen by the bombers. Her surroundings burst into piles of shrapnel as the streets exploded and caught on fire like a wave breaking on a rocky shore. She shoved a rock off from where it had pinned her wrist and felt a pain, a fiery, burning pain. She looked at it and saw that it was broken. Soar swore at her wrist and kept on running, even though her toes were bleeding and her wrist was flopping at her side like the ears of a dachshund. She flew across the street, never realizing how well she could have done in gym class, as she pumped on, burning adrenaline. Now the only area between her and the plane was the main battlefield. The blue slime, The Lovely, specked the streets and skyscrapers as if a toddler had strewn his puzzle pieces on a carpet. Mines still detonated as the city's troops advanced against the massive opposing army. Their guns rattled with glee and the glorified accounts of war were all very distant from everyone's heads.

Soar ran out into the battlefield as bullets and asphalt shook her vision and made her mind feel rusty. Enormous ash clouds hung overhead as if the sky were a volcano. She heard bullets ring next to her head on a nearby wall. She screamed and kept running. Leaping over blockades and mines, Soar felt invincible. She punched an enemy straight to the floor and could see the plane now, the propellers starting to twirl, a man outside shouting for her to hurry up, to get closer. Soar smiled.

"I'm going to make it!" she screamed.

Then, the unthinkable happened. Soar heard a whistling hiss above her as another round of The Lovely cruised downward onto the broken city. She let out a terrified scream that could've awakened the dead. Soar ran and leaped away but wasn't fast enough; the slimy blue substance netted her like a fly on a spider web. Her skin burned and melted away into the slime, and the suffocating trap muffled her unnatural screams. Her mind was tortured and twisted by the pain that kept being refreshed by the horrible substance that had a hold over her. She remembered everything bad, the falling buildings and her mind, her mind kept shutting down and restarting as wave after wave of searing pain shook her entire body, as her bones caught fire and the ashes stuck into the slime. All she could do was land roughly on to the ground. Right when Soar believed she would die, the pain abruptly stopped. And the world became a gentle calming bounce. On Earth, where Soar once had been, she no longer was. Soar Arridye had been continued.

Rafael Lopez, Grade 8
Gunston Middle School, Arlington, VA
Short Story, Silver Key

a little perspective
(excerpted)

One day, I was born. And life just went downhill from there.

Although our lives may follow completely different paths, I am not so different from you. *I* had a mother once. I, like you, once felt the warm skin and soothing beat of a heart against mine. And it felt wonderful, just for that second, that one, quick, blissful moment of complete joy and serenity. It is comforting to be with your mother as a baby. Peaceful. Some go as far as to say that nothing bad can happen to you when you're with your mom, but I beg to differ.

Moments after my birth, my brothers were snatched and ground up into pieces before my very eyes. I was grabbed by an unknown man, carrying five or six of us in each hand. We were ruthlessly thrown into a dirty, dank trunk. The next sound I heard was a disquieting squeal, and the crack of soft, young bone.

The truck came halting to a stop, and that's how I knew we had arrived. More than a sixth of us had died along the tedious journey, and the place was a bloody, worried mess. A worker hauled the door open, but before being crammed into a crate, I caught a glimpse of outside. The air was clean, fresh, and pure, something I had never quite experienced. The ground was soft and green, and I longed to stay there and graze. But the most amazing part of it all was what hung above. It was unlike anything I had ever seen before: indescribable. The iridescent object was illuminated in a beautiful, golden hue, and formed a perfect circle in the endless, blue skies. It warmed my body and my soul—giving off an optimistic sort of light. Maybe there was hope— maybe things could get better. Little did I know that object was the sun, and I would never see it again.

Upon arrival, we were transported into a small, stuffy room that seemed oddly familiar. What could I have remembered it from? Finally, the answer came to me. This place reminded me of my home, where my mother had so recently brought me into this malevolent world—what if my mother was here? This room could have very well been the place where I was born. It had the same extremely-dim lighting, the same ammonia-filled air; everything about the two rooms was practically identical– even down to the tightly-stacked cages along the walls. A surge of determination rushed through my fragile veins. *I will find my mother, whatever I do.*

But, shortly after, I was forced into a cage with five others of my size. Although the spaces between the cold, metal bars of the cage were small and the lighting was dim, I searched long and hard for my mother. I counted the cages on every row, and the beings in every cage, every day, from dawn to dusk. She had to be somewhere. But it was such a crowded room and I would lose count, and then constantly have to restart.

One day, a worker coming in left the door ajar. I could see the events taking place in the next room, and they were horrific. Hundreds of beings, looking almost identical to my mother, were hanging upside down, being reeled forward on a line, some unconscious, others cognizant. Workers stood aside, laughing, as if at play, slamming them into walls and ripping off their necks. It was gruesome, terrible, yet I watched for hours, in absolute astonishment and disbelief. One came along about an hour or so in, and, to this day, I can still see the image of her young, frightened face. She kept my gaze, staring deeply with those poor, terrified eyes, as if begging me to do something. I wished to, but there was nothing that I could do. I could barely move my legs, let alone save someone's life. She reached the end of the line, and that was the last I ever saw of her.

In my eyes, that was symbolic of something. For me, that incident signified my mother's death, for she had embodied my mother very much. So, from then on, my optimism was gone. My hope—shattered. I faced the fact that I would never see my mother again, and probably never leave this ghastly building. But giving up was disgraceful; it isn't what Mom would've wanted me to do. She would've wanted me to keep on fighting, to stay strong. For my mother's sake, I made a promise, right then and there. I would trudge on, and do whatever it took to survive. *Mother, I will stay alive.*

But, as the days wore on, this mission became harder and harder. Life was bleak, and I longed to see the sun again. It soon became apparent to me how little space we had to live our lives, and it made me miserable. I couldn't even extend my limbs without bumping into to a bar or cage-mate, and couldn't sit, stand or turn without scratching my skin on a sharp, metal edge. And although I had never experienced them, I felt there were things I was meant to do, sights I was born to see. I yearned to feel the sun shining down, the wind on my back and the luscious grass beneath my feet. Instead, we were confined to this inexorable hell.

* * *

Soon I started having babies. It was a painful process, and they all came at once, then were taken away from me within a matter of minutes. I felt the maternal need to nurture them and raise them on my own. I'd have someone to love and care for, someone who loved and cared for me. But I never got to keep any of them, so the emotional and physical ordeal outweighed the few seconds of bliss.

Eventually, they took away our food. I was despondent, starving and completely lost my sense of time. Days ran into nights, the lighting was continuously dim, and the babies kept coming. I had twice as many babies during the starvation, which made it ever more stressful and tiresome. Time slowed and I thought I might never see food again. Thoughts of my mother, fresh air, and the sun died down, and my intentions turned to eating something, anything. In retrospect, those were probably the hardest two weeks of my life.

But, in due course, my giving birth slowed, and then faded completely. The workers gave us food again, and it seemed like life was looking up. Perhaps they would set us free. So every night I dreamt of green grass, fresh air, golden sunshine, and rolling hills. Which is why I was so unprepared and utterly taken aback for the events that were to come.

They shackled us upside-down, then, without warning, dipped us into a scalding tank of electrically charged water. Many passed out in that first stage, but I was determined not to. *Whatever it takes, I'll stay alive,* I told myself. We were then attached onto a long line, slowly reeling forward. It was just like the line I had seen earlier, and, just like that one, a devastating fate awaited at the end of it. But I had to find a way out—I wasn't just going to let myself die. I could try to pull out of the shackle—no, too firmly attached. Maybe I could stop the line from moving, push a button or flip a switch—there had to be something. Whatever it took, I had to escape. I cringed as I saw someone in front of me meet her death. I can't let this happen—*I will stay alive. I will stay alive. I will stay alive–* Or do I even want to?

* * *

This is the miserable tragedy of my life, and billions of others. I, like you, deserve the right to live, behave naturally and be loved. I, too, lived in 2012 in the United States, supposedly an age of justice in a country of freedom.

But you are a human, and, unfortunately for me, *I* am a chicken.

Alessandra Lowy, Grade 9
Thomas S. Wootton High School
Rockville, MD
Persuasive Writing, Gold Key

a castle in the air
(excerpted)

The library was not of the boring, dreary kind. The sunlight was forever, and shone through the windows, making designs across the walls. They created stories of spatters of light, and spot-dappled patterns. The shelves might have gone on forever, but as of yet, forever hasn't happened. Books adorned some of the walls, but the majority of the shelf space was filled with glass vessels in which little creatures lived. Silvery wisps of pure mist and light is what they looked like. They flitted in their spaces, chirping and leaping. They were beautiful to look at.

"What are these creatures?" you may ask. They are dreams. They are waiting to be let out into the world, to visit us in our sleep. The dreams are very content flitting around, but that is not true for all the creatures in the library. In the only dark patch of shelves in the vast library, a small being watched the dreams play in the light.

* * *

The little nightmare sighed as it looked out of its glass prison. It longed to be a dream, it knew it wasn't meant for its ghastly purpose. Why must it be a nightmare? It didn't want to be frightening, it didn't feel the need to make people cry as its more nightmarish companions did. They all laughed wickedly as they thought of unleashing their horror on people. But not the little nightmare. It longingly watched as the dreams flitted happily through the light silvery glow in the chamber. It felt so alone in the world, because it wasn't really much of anything. It wasn't much of a nightmare, but not a dream either. It retreated into the depths of the container, in mourning for the life it had never had, but wished so dearly for. Many--shall I say the vast majority--of the little nightmare's days were like this. The small minority was made sunny only by the doing of one person. And that person was the Dream Librarian.

The Dream Librarian loved her job. She wished to stay in the beautiful library eternally, caring for the creatures that lived there, and making sure that the order of the library was not breached by chaos. Although she was alone, being the only human in the forever ongoing library, she didn't feel alone. She had plenty to do as the Dream Librarian. She had to make sure that all the books in the library, (although there were few) stayed in their correct place. But her favorite job, which is the reason that she ever agreed to come to the Dream Library in the first place, is that she took care of the dreams, and the nightmares, and let them out into the world when they were ready.

Whether a dream is a dream or a nightmare is a nightmare is the work of creation. No choice comes into the equation. But it is possible to change into the other type of mindscape. Dreams and nightmares, or mindscapes, come into the world every night. Someone in our world will receive them sometime in the future, when the mindscape is ready. Each mindscape embodies a different feeling, positive or negative. A dream may represent accomplishment, a nightmare may represent shame. The Dream Librarian's job was to nurture mindscapes as they grew, and to prepare them to fly into the world. Then, in the Releasing of the Mind ceremony (that is was it was formally called, but the Dream Librarian just called it "Goodbye,") which happened nightly, the mindscapes were let out into the world, where we sleep peacefully, or fitfully, depending on which mindscape visits us. Although saying goodbye was painful, the dreams made her smile, as their silvery wispy bodies surrounded her, chirping and humming. They loved her, and she loved them. But the dream corridor wasn't her favorite part of the library.

It would probably surprise you if I told you that the small, dark section of the library, where the nightmares were kept, was the brightest part of the room for the Dream Librarian. But it was. Those small dark shelves shone in her eyes. Especially the little nightmare. She had a love for that tiny swirl of darkness, a love that probably would seem strange and maybe a bit crazy to a passerby. She believed in it, and it believed in her. It thought that she was the most wonderful thing, and seemed to almost brighten to the point of becoming silvery, instead of its normal purple and black hue. She understood its desire to be a dream, and wished she could do something, but she mourned because that power was out of her hands. She and it often conversed about its pitiful plight. How she wished and wished there was some way to change the poor thing. Every shooting star that graced her sky was begged to help. To no effect. She watched as the little nightmare became more and more desperate, but also began to think that maybe it was no use, that it was stuck being a nightmare.

* * *

"Bye, my little one," The Dream Librarian called, "Find a home." She felt a wetness on her cheek, and brushed away the tear.

The little nightmare thrashed about as it tried to find a comfortable position in the whirling tunnel. Masses of colors flashed across the ceiling of the portal, and the small being was glad when the sky turned dark blue. It spent a long time gazing at the darkness, and the small pinpricks of light among it. It knew one of those stars was the library. It wished it could return to the warmth and light of its home. This darkness was overwhelming in size, covering everything. But it also knew that it must find someone in this darkness, and it flew off into the night.

It looked everywhere, in everything. Past mountains, and forests, and brightly lit urban cities. But it could not see where it could help. At one time, it saw a small girl in her bed. It also saw the tears that she cried, even in slumber. It felt drawn to her, but knew that she needed a dream, not a nightmare, and so it flew off. It looked for another location that felt right, but somehow nothing fit. It felt itself fly back to that bedroom. It watched her curiously, because she wasn't dreaming, but was still crying. It wanted to know what made her so sad. It needed to know.

The little nightmare watched as Aisling slept, and grew more and more sure that this was its purpose. It needed to help her. But it wasn't sure how. What could a nightmare do, it would make it worse. How it wished to be a dream! But it was impossible. Hadn't the Dream Librarian searched for anything, and come up with nothing? It sat suspended there, wishing more than it ever had before that it could be a dream. If only for one night, just one night, for Aisling. But this time it was special. This wish was unselfish, it didn't want to be a dream because of the comfort, but because it was the only thing that it could do to help Aisling.

It watched her jerk and thrash, but didn't notice a flash in the sky. The white light stood in contrast against the mottled blue. It flew down to the little nightmare, and the little creature felt a sharp pain, but a good sort of pain. When it looked down at itself, it was silver! It was wispy! How light it felt! The wish had come true. It was a dream, finally! It looked down at Aisling, and fell down the window ledge, right into her, where her heart was. A glow emanated from Aisling's body, and a soft smile spread across her face.

Anasuya Lyons, Grade 7
Alice Deal Middle School / Writopia Lab
Washington, DC
Short Story, Gold Key

bob mcJoe

(excerpted)

It was a regular day in Normopolis where everyone ate a normal breakfast of Normal-o's and drank a carton of Normal Juice. After that everyone went to the Norm Corp. building to work in their cubicles, everyone over the normal age of 18. All but one person:

Bob McJoe.

Bob was, like everyone, normal. But Bob didn't want to be normal, he wanted a hot pink mohawk, not a black, upside-down pudding-bowl hairstyle. And, most of all, he wanted to fly. But everyone liked the way Bob acted. He was a normal citizen, who did normal things, ate normal food, and drank normal drinks. He even dreamed normal dreams. But he always imagined, *What would it be like to be different?* He imagined himself flying through Normopolis with a big, hot pink mohawk.

He wanted to run, run far away. And he planned to do just that. He packed his bag full of necessities, like candy, his NormPad, etc. etc. Something felt odd about the whole situation, though. And then it hit him, like an Normtrak train, running at full speed. This was the first abnormal thing that had happened to him in his life.

He decided to stop at the barber shop to get that haircut he wanted. At the barber when he asked about the hairdo the barber looked confused and aghast.

"Whata you meen a peenka hot mohak," said the Italian barber.

"I mean a hot pink mohawk, a spiky, pink hairstyle going down the middle of my head. What's so complicated about that?" Bob said.

"I'ma gonna call da *polizia* you, you *ignorantone!*"

Bob started to run, as fast as he could. He could already hear the sirens. *Isn't that what a police car sounds like? Will they take me to jail?*. And then he felt a sharp pain in his left leg. *Oh no, I really am going to jail!* Then black, Stygian darkness.

In Bob's dreams induced by the midazolam tranquilizer Somno2000 gun, he flashed back to the first time he even thought of doing anything abnormal.

It all started at the Normbrary. Bob was looking through the NormBooks when he chanced upon an old book, a book so old the author's name wasn't Norm Corp.

"WHAT IS THIS!" Bob exclaimed.

"SHHHHH!" said the librarian.

Slowly Bob opened the book. It was titled *A Brief History Of the 22nd Century.* The first chapter was called "Individuality in Humans." Bob gasped, but he read on to a definition: *individuality: the quality or character of a particular person or thing that distinguishes them from others of the same kind, esp. when strongly marked.*

Suddenly Bob woke up in an office room surrounded by "guards" (or people wearing gray cargo pants and t-shirts with a sticker plastered on their chest saying "POLICE.")

"What is your name, criminal," a guard spat at Bob.

"My name is Bob, Eojcm Bob," Bob answered.

The guards looked incredulously at him.

"It's Icelandic," said Bob.

"Oh," said the guards.

"Where were you on the night of May 5th, 2201?" yelled one of the guards.

"At my house," lied Bob.

"Then why did we find you at the BARBER SHOP asking for an ILLEGAL PINK MOHAWK!?!" As the guard ranted, spittle flew from the his mouth.

"I dd-don't kn-know," said Bob.

"He's lying," said another guard. "I can tell by the stammering."

"C'mon boys. That's all I needed to know," said a guard who looked like the leader.

"We're finally going to the Norm Corp. HQ," said another.

"Noooooo!" exclaimed Bob.

"Shut UP!" said the leader. And then he elbowed Bob in the temple.

"Unh," Bob groaned.

In his forcefully induced sleep he recalled what happened after he opened *A Brief History Of the 22nd Century.*

"Oh my Norm!" exclaimed Bob.

"SHHHHH!" said the librarian. Ignoring her, Bob read on:

"People are possibly the most diverse species...different in almost any way...always changing... no one is the same..."

"What world is this in, a fantasy?!" Bob whispered so as to not attract attention.

Suddenly Bob woke up with a gasp, slung over someone's shoulder.

"Where am I ?" he questioned.

"Inside an elevator," said one of the 'policemen'. And then Bob remembered all that had happened.

"Noooooo!" he groaned.

"Do you want me to knock you out again?" said the leader.

"Please, no!"

"Then SHUT UP!"

As he awaited his fate, thinking of what would happen, the elevator suddenly stopped, and the door opened with a hiss. Bob saw a normal office room filled with cubicles.

"This is the Norm Corp. HQ?" Bob said, incredulous at its averageness.

"Yep, very normal, unlike you," one of the guards answered.

At first when he entered no one noticed him, and why should they, it was probably an employee coming from another level, but then an employee stood up and gasped. In Normopolis no one gasps unless they either lost their breath or something strange has or is happening.

"Who is that boy?"

"What did he do?"

"Are those the POLICE!?"

All these questions were ignored like a blade of grass in a meadow as the 'policemen' shoved their way through the crowd of shocked employees. By the time the group got their way through the crowd, a quarter of the employees were sprawled on the ground.

"POLICE COMING THROUGH," bellowed the leader, like we didn't already know that. The 'policemen' led Bob up a stairwell and into a spacious room overlooking the Normopolis skyline.

"I have been waiting for you," said a deep voice that was obviously used to being obeyed. Bob shivered as he heard the voice of none other than the great Joe Jim, head of Norm Corp. Joe Jim is a middle-aged man who has average length black, pudding-bowl shaped hair and pitch-black eyes. Those eyes, like black holes of normal-mediocre-averageness, sucking in all the abnormalness from the world. Nothing can escape. Nothing except... Bob McJoe.

"You have two choices," said Jim. "Choice one: go through a slow and painful torture where the agony will keep you on the brink of death, then heal you, then rinse and repeat until you are normal, which is never," he said cruelly. "Choice two: die, mua ha ha ha ha ha!"

"I choose…neither!" exclaimed Bob.

He then proceeded to defenestrate himself out of a 5,000 norm tall building.

John Smith was being chased by the police on his jetpack stolen from the black market when he suddenly heard a scream:

"For Abnormalityyyyyyyyyy!" Bob screamed as someone who was about to die, which he was, when suddenly he landed on a boy about his age flying on a jetpack.

"Oof!" they both exclaimed.

Bob's momentum pushed the boys down, just missing a Somno2000 gun's tranquilizing midazolam dart and landing in a dumpster.

"Owwwwwwww," said Bob.

"SHHHHH," said John.

The police cars passed, completely missing the two boys.

5,000 norms away, one of the 'policemen' said,

"He's dead, Jim."

Marcus McKee, Grade 7
Westland Middle School / Writopia Lab
Bethesda, MD
Short Story, Honorable Mention

hebrew school
(excerpted)

Maybe if I hadn't gone to Hebrew school I would be a better Jew. Maybe if I hadn't gone I would believe in God. Isn't that what everyone wants, really? To believe, to live for something and die for something? For faith, or for truth, or for love. Something to hold onto, a life raft in this great big rushing sea of ours. And in this huge, beautiful sea, I am drowning.

The waves of doubt and cynicism crash over me, the next one appearing just as I catch my breath. And the worst of it, the thought that makes me want to just sink and sink and sink until there is nothing. The thought that these doubts are my own, born and raised in *my* mind. They are no one else's, and they are inescapable. How can you escape from yourself? So I wait and wait for answers.

I don't wish for death, since I don't know what death is. Heaven? Peace? Those who have faith in God can hope for peace. Those who have faith in science can know there is an end. Those who have neither are doomed to wait, and they are doomed to never know what they are waiting for. Because of my own skeptical heart, I will wait. And while I wait, I will go to Hebrew school.

* * *

"Today we are discussing Job."

I try not to groan. In the language of Hebrew school teachers, the word "discussion" is synonymous with the word "lecture." Thalia (we call teachers by their first names here) writes "Job" on the blackboard. On the left side of the class, people start their weekly routine of doodling on other people's arms with sharpies, checking Facebook on half-concealed phones, and slowly falling into a kind of stupor. One boy already has his head in his arms, fast asleep. I am immediately envious. The girl sitting next to him starts drawing tiny hearts on his neck. Okay, less envious. But I bet it still beats hearing about Job.

The right-hand side of the class obviously disagrees. They are all staring at Thalia with varying degrees of rapture on their faces. A girl I know named Julia has actually begun taking notes. (It should be noted that the left-hand side of the class vastly outnumbered the right-hand side.)

I sit in the middle, with several other teenagers whose expressions range between a. mildly unhappy b. very unhappy c. mutinous d. suicidal, and one e. murderous. But he always looks like that, so I'm not including him on the official scale. My mood was probably a c. today, but it was quickly spiraling down towards d.

"Who can tell me about Job?"

I knew that this was just a question to give Thalia a platform for her oncoming sermon. Julia and Matthew both shot their hands into the air. Thalia studiously ignored them.

"Tyler?" she asked hopefully. Tyler was the sleeping boy who was being written on by the boys next to him. It was hard to tell from my seat, but it looked like they were scribbling obscenities on his arm in permanent marker.

Tyler started awake. "Whaa? Is it over yet?" There was a chorus of badly concealed snickers from the right hand side of the class and most of the middle table, too.

Thalia gave him a look that would have frozen the Eternal Flame. She looked like a charging lion in heels and cheap makeup.

"No. I wanted you to tell me who Job is."

Tyler looked terrified. He glanced at the door, as if considering escape routes in case Thalia decided to pounce.

"He was a guy... in the Torah?" he hazarded. When he realized this was not an acceptable answer, he continued, looking more desperate with every word. "Um. I think he. Um." He looked around the room in a silent plea for help. Thalia decided to take mercy on Tyler.

"Brian, why don't you help Tyler out?" she asked, turning to the boy sitting two seats down from me. His face was currently in an expression I did not give a letter on the scale, because the only face I have ever seen it on is Brian's. It looked like someone had tried to make a sarcastic face while squinting at a bright light. It did not do much to improve his looks.

He appeared to be considering this question carefully. He squinted even more and tilted his head to one side, giving him the appearance of a rabid, freckle-covered hamster. He remained like this for a good forty-five seconds before Thalia gave up and turned to Julia. Brian looked mildly proud at his successful avoidance of the question. Tyler went back to sleep. I managed to tune out the rest of Julia's answer and remained in this semi-conscious state until we were allowed to stampede out of the classroom like the Israelites fleeing Egypt.

* * *

The really depressing thing about Hebrew school is the teachers. I wonder if this is what they expected when they became teachers. I'm sure they didn't grow up with this as their life's ambition. Maybe they wanted to become rabbis and never made it. All I know is that they don't do it for the money. (I don't even know if they get paid. I'm pretty sure at least two of them live in the staff lounge.)

I wonder if they believe they're getting through to some of us, just some, carrying on a tradition even if the rest of us are moving on. I wonder if they've realized by now that I'm a lost cause, that they might as well send me home early and concentrate on teaching the ones who actually want to be taught. It's probably too late for me, the cynicism has set in too deep. Maybe it's taken over the little piece of me that always believed, spreading like a parasite until everything has been eaten away. If you looked at an x-ray of me, my bones would form a question mark.

What makes me the most frustrated is being preached at. When people start lecturing you about the Torah like they have all the wisdom in the world, and they have generously decided to bestow it on you. Like they have figured it all out, like it's inscribed in huge block letters right above your head. Hebrew school teachers are the world champions of sermons. It is their job after all. But worst of all is the way they use religious writing as a tool, a means to an end. The way they twist it and bend it to fit into some prescribed moral or lesson. It makes me feel like I'm being brainwashed, and also that I'm becoming paranoid.

* * *

"And that is why God sent the great flood. Any questions?"

We were sitting around a dark blue rug in the shape of a slightly squashed circle. The walls were plastered with posters saying things like "Alef first, Tav last, Always be on time for class!" Abe, the first grade teacher, was sitting cross-legged and completely oblivious to the fact that we were way too old to be sitting in a circle on the floor. Most of the class was either listening to Abe or staring into space, their eyes glazed over and their heads in their hands. Another girl whose name probably started with 'L' raised a hand.

"I don't really get it. What happened to all the animals who didn't get on the ark? Did they go somewhere else?" L asked.

Abe looked suddenly uncomfortable. He ran a huge hand along his receding hairline. "Um. Not exactly, no."

Jennifer McLish, Grade 9
Maret School/Writopia Lab
Washington, DC
Personal Essay, Silver Key

rooftops

"Tell me what you see"
The doctor would say to me.
And I'd tell him.
And he'd say there was nothing wrong with me.
Check something on his clipboard
And send me home.
I knew there was something wrong with me
But no one would ever notice.
"What did you see?"
My father would ask of me.
And I'd tell him nothing.
Because my mother would be heartbroken
If I told her what I really saw him doing
With that woman who was not her.
On the kitchen counter.
And he'd say I was alright, kid
That nothing was wrong with me.
And he'd send me away,
On back to bed.
I knew there was something wrong with me
But no one would ever notice.
"What do you see?"
My conscience would whisper to me.
And I'd look.
And I'd see below me.
And I'd tell myself
That I saw the little girl
Running with the balloon
That I saw the business man
With the dapper suit
That I saw the beautiful woman

With the nice handbag
That I saw the clown
With the swift juggling hands.
But that little girl's balloon would burst
And red would pour from it
And the pieces would fall apart.
And she'd cry.
And the business man would go home
And his wife's skin would burn
Like the iron she had set too high
Much too high for the suit to withstand
And she'd cry.
And that beautiful woman
With the nice handbag
Could only afford it because of the crime
No one knew she had committed upon her husband.
She had cried.
And that clown— that wretched clown
Used his hands
Not only to juggle pins
But to commit a heinous sin
which is the reason for all mothers' worries.
And the children would cry...
And I'd say there was something very wrong with me.
That I should be seeing any of this in the first place
And speaking of these people
In such a horrid way.
But no one had ever noticed.
No one had ever cared.
Not as much as their clipboards,
their women,
their balloons,
their suits,
their handbags,
their hands...

And that is why I wrote these words to you before I jumped.

Josalyn Montgomery, Grade 12
Charles Herbert Flowers High School
Springdale, Maryland
Poetry, Silver Key

duty of the firstborn

My lineage traces back on a long, winding path to Vietnam and is considered royal. In my bloodline, I am the firstborn of my family and am part of the first generation born in the United States. My great grandmother was a princess called Anh Ngọc Nữ Toh Tân Công, sister of the emperor that ruled one of the last Vietnamese dynasties. For my great-grandmother, the long name came with infinite wealth to last her eternally, had she been able to live that long. Based on the only surviving photograph of her, she was quite beautiful with unusually large eyes and a tall height. Instead of marrying another prince to increase her social status, my great-grandmother chose to marry a teacher because she valued intelligence over material goods, a motto ingrained into my ancestor's blood that today roars through my veins.

In my family, intelligence is the key to life that is meant to be pursued. No intelligence means no capability to think and make sensible judgments. The environment I was nurtured in taught me that it was my duty to achieve beyond the horizon because this is what humans were born for, and to reach outwards and absorb everything within touch because the brain has no limits. Obstacles are meant to be pummeled, not overleapt. Unfortunately, the bar that sets the standards in my family has fallen unbelievably low.

When the Vietnam Civil War swept through like the bubonic plague, it took hold of fathers and eldest sons, forcing elementary students to drop out of school to help out with families. As a result, my parents never received the full education they deserved, and today still struggle with basic English. It has been approximately thirty years since they immigrated to America. Currently, my father works three jobs and is in the process of opening his own company. Feeding five hungry mouths, including himself, is not an easy task, so taking time off to chase a better education is nearly impossible. What is the effect? He lives through me. The family standard bar that the Vietnam Civil War chucked aside is pressing against my shoulders, dependent on my strength to lift it back up. It was at the tender age of eleven when I realized this, and I did what any teenager does best: rebel.

Even when I rebelled, it was mostly internal, as going against my sense of duty is like willingly labeling myself average. On account of pride, I did not want to be named in front of my younger cousins and future generations as the person who gave up her duty and could not live up to the family's standards. As a result, questions constantly troubled my mind, churning in their bottled prison. Why did I have to bear the responsibility of setting the family standard? My parents said it was because I am the eldest child. Why is it that whenever I pushed a task aside, there was always some teasing and criticism? My grandparents and parents said it is because they want the best for me. Was it the best for me or the best for them? Who is living this life that is supposed to be mine? Was I a puppet to control? I certainly hoped not! Unfortunately, this was only the first rebelling stage I went through.

The second was frustration. It swept in like a tornado and engulfed me like a tsunami. The winds blew me into pieces, and waves congealed those pieces into a disfigured blob, amorphous and thus unable to maintain a solid identity. *What was I supposed to do with all these responsibilities?* I didn't know what to do but ignore the situation and delve into a world of books, becoming a quiet and brooding child.

After the frustration came a bittersweet mix of anger and desperation. I felt like I was alone. Of course there were plenty of other blood-related firstborns in my generation, but they were all younger than me. I was the firstborn of firstborns and therefore the pressure rested squarely on me to set that annoying bar. At this point, my grades were perfect as can be but even so, internally I was being burned raw by fiery flames. I became tired mentally. I felt lackadaisical, as if I had become a robot, programmed by the elders around me. I didn't want to pretend that nothing was wrong and that I was happy to accept my duty, but to my chagrin, as a flawed, egoistical human, I didn't want to admit defeat either.

Soon it was the season of dying leaves, and creeping in with Jack Frost's chills was an apocalypse. I was officially a high school student. My time was running out. I had four years to decide what I wanted to do and set my future in stone. Again, because of my pride and my family's beliefs, I knew that the moment I chose a path, there would be no going back. Much to my dissatisfaction, I ended up pouring more fuel into my anger by being the obedient firstborn, listening to my parents and circling the classes they expressed more enthusiasm for. The rest of my ninth grade year was the numbest I had ever felt.

Although I was fully aware I wasn't getting anything done by ignoring my dilemma, I found myself relieved when ninth grade came to an end, even if it meant I had three years left. By this point, I was exhausted. My mind felt as if it had been charred raw, and everything I did felt sluggish. I spent my summer lounging in my grandparent's house, playing chess with my cousins in front of the altar of my great-grandparents. I remember sneaking glances at my great-grandmother's smiling portrait and comparing it to my great-grandfather's plain face. I just couldn't comprehend it. Why would a princess pick such a plain husband, disgrace the family, and still be able to set a legacy? As I sat pondering this question, I absentmindedly won every chess game against my cousins. My grandfather complimented me. He said I had my great-grandmother's blood talent. If he was right, then in what aspects was I like my grandmother?

Quickly rerunning over my life, the answer came slowly after three more chess games. I realized that my great-grandmother, being a princess, must have gone through the same bitterness and anger that I did when it was time for her to decide how and with whom she wanted to live her future. Both she and I were battling against our desires and our duties. My mind, miraculously still functioning, reeled in revelation, shocked that I had not figured this out sooner. My great-grandmother was able to set a legacy because in the end, she had listened to what she wanted, and not to what her parents wanted. Thus, with a gentle tap of my queen and a checkmate, I decided to channel my great-grandmother and follow my heart.

In the three months before tenth grade started, I grew alarmingly. Not in height, but mentally. My heart took control and gently turned my mind a 180 before recharging it. My thoughts ran clear, sweetly pure, and clean. No longer did I react with distaste when my parents or any other adult reprimanded me or gave their opinions on how to succeed. Instead, if my instincts deemed the advice useful, I listened carefully and tucked it away. I made decisions based on my own experiences and what I wanted, instead of my parents' experiences. I did what my gut told me was right.

When I look back, I think that had I trusted myself more, I wouldn't have wasted five years of my life in constant denial. Today, I walk forward with my head held high, determined to fulfill my duty as the firstborn of firstborns. I am slowly reestablishing the academic standard that future generations will exceed and improve on. I walk the invisible path my ancestors paved with their blood, the same blood that caused my great-grandmother to choose her husband. Are you proud of me, my ancestors?

Mimi Nguyen, Grade 10
Thomas Jefferson High School
Alexandria, Virginia
Personal Essay, Silver Key

i found him in the ballot box
(excerpted)

i. *Tripoli, Libya, August 2000*

We jumped up and down on the bed we shared
every summer for four years, frail bodies colliding with
the walls and the jetlag that kept us awake, our laughs
reverberating through the empty hallways and the
flourishing courtyard beyond. It was a summer of
innocence, of horses named Azeeza[1] and dusty roads
and seaweed allergies, of cigarette smoke and tuna
sandwiches and well water driven in by my uncle every
week[2]. It was late, too late for the two little girls
bouncing up, down, up, down, and my grandfather
came over to tuck us in, playfully stern as he always was
when we were children. We were mock-insulting each
other by then, tossing around the words we thought
would simultaneously be the most ridiculous and the
most disgusting, our tiny voices making the scene all
the more comical.

You're kaka[3]*!* I slung, receiving a laughing *Well, you're
gidaaf*[4]*!* in return. *You're Gaddafi!* I burst out, our giggles
filling the room. *Gaddafi's gidaaf, Gaddafi's gidaaf,
Gaddafi's gidaaf,* we chanted, our voices bouncing higher

---

[1] Arabic for 'reasured one.'

[2] When Gaddafi's self-interested tyranny hit the hardest, clean drinking
water was the first thing to go. Trash collection went next (you have no
idea what the streets began to look like).

[3] Poop in Arabic children's slang (not considered profane).

[4] In Libyan Arabic, *gidaaf* means vomit. Its phonetic resemblance to the
name Gadaffi, of course, was not lost to us as children (they are not in fact
etymologically related).

and higher, product of a first amendment childhood, the springs in the bed creaking with our leaps.

My grandfather's face changed when he entered and heard us, contorted, molded with emotions I would not know until later, until after my world dissolved its sugar coat and strange men shattered two towers, countless lives, and the identities of Muslim Americans the world over: until fear became commonplace and anger abundant.

Quiet! The police will come for you! Quick, under the covers, quick, go to bed, that's right, don't say it again.

We didn't understand, but how could we? We were not born to fear other human beings, to quake at the very mention of their names. Besides, he was *jaddu* [5]: he did not fear anything, and he knew best. So we lay down, and we waited for the *mu'athin* [6] to give the call to prayer as we dozed, because in a country where it seemed as though He was nowhere, we found God in those words.

ii. Washington, D.C., January 2011

I first heard while in Arabic class, taking to heart the heritage of peoples too-long dormant, too-long oppressed. We were studying the dark age that was pre-Islamic Arabia — its culture, its traditions — an Arabia that was too close for comfort to the one we saw (or, rather, didn't see) on our television screens, untouched by progress. We spoke of change, and upheaval, and tumult, but we had no idea what this talk would foretell, what happenings were afoot.

---

[5] Grandfather in Libyan Arabic (and some other dialects).
[6] Person who gives the Muslim call to prayer. In Tripoli (and most countries with Muslim majorities), these calls are made from every mosque and can be heard from any part of the city. Prayers are 5 times a day; the one referred to hear is the Fajr prayer, held at dawn.

It was her son who first told us, face lit up as he screamed of a future none of us could anticipate, as he yelled with a pride we did not know could ever exist.

Egypt's done it, Egypt's done it! he cried, *They've started their revolution!*

And we just looked at each other, Tunisia on our tongues – for we had regarded her as an anomaly – but our hearts at a loss, not risking a word, not allowing all that she portended to slip out for fear of losing what (we dared not wish) could be. And so we counted the dead as they came, we tracked their chants and their stances, *ash-sha'b yureed isqaat an-nitham*[7]. We heard them, and we rallied and we hoped, created our own Tahrir Square right in Lafayette[8], collected photos as they trickled in, shuddered at tear gas and laughed at Mubarak, cried at the circle of Christians protecting the Muslims as they prayed because in the midst of the funerals and the shouts, the cacophony of conflict, when it seemed as though He was nowhere, we found God in that gathering.

iii. Washington, D.C., February 2011

I had just come home when I found out, Al Jazeera blasting and phones ringing, sounds mingling with the tense discussions of half of the DC Libyan community, all gathered in our house. It was February 17th, a date that would later be displayed proudly across the fourth largest country in its continent, but for now one that was frightening in its tumult, breathtaking in its significance. Benghazi, legendary hotbed of Libyan

---

[7] "The people want to bring down the regime," a slogan popularized in protests across the region.

[8] For those of you who aren't from DC/don't go to protests, Lafayette Square is where they are held in front of the White House.

dissent, was erupting, and all we could do was watch, mesmerized, teetering at the edge of our seats. It was the start of something big, and we could feel it in the air, still reverberating with the ouster of Mubarak, the exile of Ben Ali. But Gaddafi? The mad dog of the Middle East[9], subject of a collective nation's nightmares for forty-two consecutive years? We dared not hope, for 42 years of Gaddafi had taught us that that was futile; but two weeks of our fight for freedom unwove those lies and freed our faith, spirits flying and hearts on the front lines.

I watched on tenterhooks as our rebels were slaughtered, following live-action news in hallways after biology classes, counting the dead, (losing count of the dead,) decrying rampant inhumanities to unfeeling friends in play-by-plays that would have awed even the most seasoned of sports reporters (friends whom I would later abandon because I cannot stomach apathy in the face of violence). We started our weekly protests, every Saturday afternoon, Lafayette becoming the canvas on which we painted our convictions, this time the green, black, and red of our very own Martyrs' Square. We launched ourselves into our own government, ultimately securing a no-fly zone and NATO support[10]. But still we held vigils to remember those whom we had lost — stories, old and new, trickling out in a steady stream of astonishment: a great-uncle who was a pilot, thought lost in flight, actually

---

[9] A designation that I hate (how can you lump the incredible diversity of the region into a simple designation like 'Middle East?') from a man whom I hate (cue the sounds of a diminished middle class).

[10] Both results of vigorous campaigning on the part of the DC Libyan-American community, in which my father played a leading role — so I often heard of the discussions around the issue before they were made public, making the time (for my family, anyway) all the more nerve-wracking.

ordered to cover up a Gaddafi murder and then sent to his own death 30 years ago; shelling on my grandfather's street, the path which I had taken to the mosque every day as a child; another great-uncle, beaten on the side of the road and only spared death by the wails of his son, thirteen years old and terrified. It was a time of no restraint: we, the young, were timidly discovering what it meant to have pride in a heritage we had heretofore neglected and they, the old, were solidifying the hopes they had had for decades, my grandparents remembering the homeland that they had once loved. I was once told that age becomes a library when books are banned, its tears the ink with which we preserved civilizations – and when the path was the most bloody, and it seemed as though He was nowhere, I found God in those tears.

iv. *Washington, D.C., July 4, 2011*

It was Independence Day at the National Harbor, my heart pulsating *red, white, blue* as fervently as my grandfather's beat *green, red, black*, my sky filling with the flames of a 200-year-old freedom, his with the flashes of unceasing NATO airstrikes. We stared at the display, eyes flickering between fireworks and the news on our phone screens – minds bedazzled, hearts troubled (or was it hearts bedazzled, minds troubled? I still don't know). It was under those lights that I whispered to my father, voice trembling, *imagine if the revolution were to succeed today; then our liberty would be two-fold*. And when the two skies were bursting with light, and it seemed as though He was nowhere, I found God in that night.

v. *Sousse, Tunisia, August 2011*

It was a city fit to bursting with refugees[11], hotels fully booked and not a leasable apartment in sight, Libyans on every street corner: talking, smoking, playing cards. The air was suffused with anticipation, the aroma of sea salt laced with a whiff of hope here, a promise of unity there. It smelled of old colliding with new, of the fresh paint that replaced the *Ben Ali*s written all over the city with symbols of revolution on roads and signs and livelihoods (faint imprints still showing through). It was a boisterous month, the news we heard from across the border tempered only by the fervent prayers of Libyan and Tunisian alike, heads side by side on the ground, makings of a Ramadan like no other.

I defined dread that month, found it in the pauses between news reports, in the hours between phone calls from my father, performing surgeries on the battle lines in Libya (*Is your bulletproof vest still intact? Are you getting enough food?*), in the innocent questions of children from whom I had to turn away (three years old and asking, *When are the bombs coming back?*). It was a dread mitigated by excitement, by the spirit that fastened us to Al Jazeera and played resurgent anthems as the green, red, and black waved from pirate ship rides at late-night amusement parks.

Such was the excitement that possessed us when Tripoli was freed, that filled the nighttime streets of Sousse with the energy of victory, people shouting and children clapping, that festooned the populace – Tunisian and Libyan alike – with the songs and symbols

---

[11] My grandfather's third time as a refugee to date. All three times from Gaddafi and his regime.

of our bid for freedom (the music a revolution in and of itself). We drove down highways and side roads, my body half-in the car, half-out; my mind half-elated, half-thrilled, reeling with possibility, reveling in the beginning of the end of this struggle. It was not until later, not until my uncle told me that this was the first time he had seen patriotism touch the hearts of Libyans, the first time he had felt such pride himself, that I understood, tears in my eyes. And on that night, when we were at the cusp of a new era, and it seemed as though He was everywhere, I found God in that pride.

Anwar Omeish, Grade 11
Thomas Jefferson High School
Alexandria, VA
Personal Essay, Gold Key

photographs
(excerpted)

Zoom out. See the pale houses shrinking, the sky widening into a vast blank sheet behind you, drowning the viewfinder in the color of impending rain. From here the world is small enough to disappear with a twist of the lens, unfocused into shades of tired grey, the city as if seen behind raindrops clotted on a dusty window. Even the sun - weak now in shapeless yellow, its watery footprints dissolving into the clouds. The snap of the shutter is sharp over the cough of distant thunder. Squat down on the hill, sip your cold coffee, throw on your wrinkled jacket. The storm is distant, building on the other side of the camera. Turn the flash off and hum over the rain as you wait for the horizon to blur, for the whip of the trees as the lightning begins.

After a few years, the skies had all become the same. Once he would have analyzed the stripes of shadow, squatted over the grass and imagined the angle that might have turned it into something like art. He was too old now, though, too tired of searching even if he could have. He had gotten two screws in his knee the year before, three years back a titanium bolt drilled into the joint of his bad hip. He wondered idly whether they would just keep on replacing him, the doctors with their sterilized gloves and lab coats and air, a nail here and a rivet there until nothing of his own was left. Steel bones, iron veins. He was sure they could do it.

He raised the camera, lowered it. His daughter had told him again that morning he should retire. He knew that tone of voice, the one he had so often used with her. Disapproval layered over that condescending lilt, like he was too old to know what was best for him, too blind to realize that the magazine didn't use half of his shots anymore, that the young college photographers had replaced him and the obsolete cameras he refused to give away. If there was one thing he couldn't take it was that, that exaggerated patience, that painfully loud voice that they all used with him now. The editors would introduce him to the new employees, pointing out his experience like he was some exhibit, a relic of the times of typewriters and newspaper boys. He could see the blankness behind their grave nods, their hasty handshakes. In their minds they had already moved on – a job at a bigger publication, a bigger paycheck and some travel, later their own studios or a bit of freelance work.

It had all seemed so simple then, so certain. He had been as good as them, maybe better. A few awards, some exhibitions. It had taken very little to convince him that he was destined for greatness. What had he wanted? To change the world, probably. Maybe he even could have...it didn't matter much anymore. He looked up from the viewfinder at the gaping clouds, the houses shivering wanly as if some careless editor had teased the exposure too high. One more photograph, that was all he needed.

The rain began to fall, and he realized he had forgotten an umbrella. Sound bounced hollowly from the sunken clouds, the thunder strangely disjointed, a distant roar in his ears like music heard from underwater. He had done a few ocean shoots before, photos of some schooner that had sunk off the coast. They'd removed the bodies when he got there, but it had still made him uneasy – the press of the water dense and silent, fighting the movement of his lungs. It had been cold, too cold, down there. He could too easily imagine being trapped in the cabin as the poor tourists had been, breathing in the stale air as the water rose around their feet, clawing toward the hatch wedged shut by the weight of the fallen mast. When he reached the ship algae was weaving between the slats of the wooden ladders, wide-eyed minnows flitting through the open doors. The kelp had clung to his wetsuit even after he surfaced, wrapped around his limbs like strands of glistening hair. He always hated doing photographs like that, afterwards, when the only thing left was the wreckage and that hollowness in the pit of his stomach. He'd never taken another picture under water.

The raindrops clotting on his face were suddenly too close to a thinner echo of the sea, and uneasily he brushed them away. The editor had called him yesterday, given him a small assignment for a ten-photograph portfolio to be crammed against a margin somewhere, fill one of the pages abandoned by another advertiser. He'd done five of them at a construction site downtown, a few shots of welders spraying sparks against the summer breeze, shadowed cranes swiveling over the building's skeleton. Four more now – he was too tired to coax another picture from the darkening town, too cautious to risk the camera in the rain. One left.

It would be late, just a bit, but they would only nod and take the folder as they always did now. Once he would have had his pay for the project docked, a lecture at the very least. It had all been so urgent, then, so precise. He realized he must have loved it – a second between a cover shot and a wasted roll of film, the relief as he slid the assignment across the desk to the irate publishers inhaling thick cigars.

In the field he had relished the instant snap of the shutters, the single moment plucked sharp and clear from chaos. It was always the same frame that he worked for: the deer twisting in mid-leap a moment before the gun goes off, the taut helpless stare of the convicted as the judge announces the verdict. He knew this, the silence before the final motion, the instant when the fate was known and sealed and left to the terrible empty wait. What drew him to it? Maybe the faces, so raw, so human then after hope and illusion had been stripped away. The feeling – the strange force that pulled at the tips of his fingertips, the heat that prickled like a sparkler lit beneath his skin. It had drawn him across continents, this hunger, and he pretended it had left him now so the folder of empty pictures digging into the corner of his briefcase didn't push him onto the next plane to anywhere. He was too old for that.

The click of the shutter bounces from the walls, and you turn to frame another snapshot, waiting for another photograph to push itself from the blur of faces. You used to flick your eyelids shut sometimes, hold a single image and try to twist it into your synapses. Small things – the colored shadows your birthday balloons painted across the sidewalk, your grandmother's face as you kissed her goodnight. They were the moments that slipped into the edges of your favorite dreams, the seconds you wished your mind was a camera that could keep them there forever. You had chosen then to be the observer. It was only later, far later, that you realized in real life the one behind the lens was never in the picture.

Gillian Page, Grade 9
Georgetown Day School / Writopia Lab, Washington, DC
Short Story, Gold Key

four ways she may have turned to stone

One

Gradually, like a long drawn-out sigh. So slow she barely noticed it at first, and even then only in glimpses – the stiffness of a single strand of marble hair, a new paleness in the sharp bones of her cheeks, a certain sluggishness to her feet as she walked around the house. Everyday things began to take longer, sometimes without her noticing. Brushing a stray hair from her eyes could take hours. When he called her to invite her to lunch, she spent a day deciding where they should go. He kept the phone by his ear the whole time and wrote down each syllable on a faded yellow sheet of paper, combined them in thin columns until they became words, deciphered the meaning behind every slow intake of breath. She never showed up at the café. He waited a week for her to call and explain, then came to her house. He found her standing in the kitchen. The skin of her arm sparkled in the thin stream of sunlight that shined through the window, crisscrossed with mazes of blue stone veins. Her marble hand was poised in midair as if waiting. She had just finished putting down the phone.

Two

With every word she spoke another part of her turned to stone. *Hello,* she said one morning to the mailman as he dropped the day's letters through the slot in her door, and her pinky toe hardened and turned to marble in her slippers. *Water,* spoken to the waiter at the diner down the street, was her left wrist. *No,* to her best friend, was her hip. *I love you,* to her boyfriend, was both ears and the sole of her right foot. *Why* was the sharp ridge of her collarbone. *We shouldn't* was the three smallest knuckles of her left hand. *Tomorrow* was the arch of her right cheekbone. The last words she spoke were *Stay with me.* Her two knees and her jaw; she did not call for him to come back and he did not turn around as he walked away from her, his footsteps echoing like slammed doors in the pools of stagnant water the rain left on the street.

Three

The bottle said *Drink me;* she took a sip and was small again, her arms as thin and delicate as the bones of birds, and she laughed at her frailty. The cake, chocolate crumbs on a small seaglass platter, said *Eat me.* She didn't care much for chocolate but did as it asked and suddenly she was a tree, so large she could barely move without breaking through the walls, and it made her feel old and powerful and a little bit scared. But slowly her legs shrank back to normal like wilting flowers. Like a child growing backwards, she deflated and found herself alone and small in that dark room. Somewhere far away she thought she could hear someone calling her name, a faint voice, searching. She wasn't ready to be found. And so she stepped back into the dank coldness of that room and said, *What next?* The paper dropped from above her, the way she had fallen so long ago, dipping and twirling in its lightness, and she grabbed it out of the air and read: *What do you want?* She took another breath, cold and fresh like air after swimming. *To feel like this forever,* she said into the darkness of the room.

This time it was a box, smooth and round like the seed of some giant fruit. *Touch me*, it said, and she reached out her hand.

Four

Three years passed and she met him in the supermarket. She was in the cereal aisle searching for her roommate's favorite type of oatmeal when someone came up behind her and she looked up for just a second to say excuse me and there were his eyes. A light grey blue just as she remembered, like the sky after rain. He ran his hand through his hair and cleared his throat and said *hey* to the box of Cheerios behind her head. And she opened her mouth to say something back but her jaw froze and the words turned to dust in her throat and she could do nothing but stare into those rainy eyes with her pale marble ones, blank and expressionless as stone.

Rachel Page, Grade 9
Woodrow Wilson High School / Writopia Lab
Washington, DC
Flash Fiction, Gold Key

days like water

When you feel like drowning in the bath,
call me and I will
make a sad joke about it, I guess
drive over to your house to pull you out of the water
and when I feel like running a red light on the way
there, and I call you, you'll say
"Don't do it, love,
if you've nothing to live for,
then that's nothing to die for"

I will stare straight into the stoplight until it tints my
vision red and clench my knuckles around the steering
wheel. I'll say, "Don't call me love, I'm not a little girl
and this isn't love, this is two similar souls clinging to
each other in an ocean of indifference to keep each
other from drowning, except maybe that's all love is
anyway

how would I know."
Because my motto is who needs love when you've got
textbooks
because who gets love when you're like we are
because I'm just your love,
but we're not in love
we just plan on having the same scars.

and the light will turn green and I'll drive to your house,
staying on the phone with you the whole way. By the
time I get there, you will actually already have gotten
out of the bath, and you'll be wearing the bathrobe your
fourth boyfriend got you, which you kept even though

you said it was a creepy gift to buy someone you weren't married to, and which has now lasted longer than he did. I'll make you put on real clothes and sit down at the kitchen table while I find your medication in the kitchen cabinet and lay all the pills out on the kitchen counter, counting them and checking dates obsessively, trying to make sure you haven't swallowed any

as though I would know, as though I am responsible and over grilled cheese sandwiches and the sound of your hair drying I'll say

"This is possibly better than suicide." Pouring the milk, I'll add, "I have never tried suicide, and therefore I am unable to verify this claim, but I suspect that this is better."

and you'll say
"I'm sure it is, love."
and I'll say, don't call me love, this isn't love, it's just enough to live on.

Cassie Paris, Grade 12
H-B Woodlawn High School
Arlington, VA
Poetry, Silver Key

re: history of love

1. THE MEANING OF DREAMS THAT KEEP ME UP AT NIGHT.

I was falling. The dark sky was empty but there I was falling through it. It had been a rough day and before I'd gone to bed I had swallowed two ibuprofen. The bottle warned against taking more than six in any twenty-four hour period, and I had to resist the urge to disobey this. Yet I did resist, but here in this world built by my imagination I am falling and I don't know why.

2. I TRIED TO COMMIT SUICIDE ONCE.

The note I left read: "I've made many mistakes and this will be my last one. God forgive me."
But when my lungs were burning and I was about to release my last bubble of air to the surface of the water, the door opened and someone screamed.

3. I WAS YOUNG THEN.

And being older now you can say that I have a broader view of the world. Getting out of that hospital, and away from others like me, was simply a blessing my knees were too weak to thank God for. Before any of that, I would like to think I was well thought of; people called, asked to meet up. But now people are afraid to look into the eyes of a true sinner; this is something that never made sense to me because how are you ever able to look at yourself in the mirror? Or is it that people just don't look hard enough?

4. MY MOTHER ALWAYS TOLD ME TO NEVER BE TOO NICE.

But things changed. I know she can't shake that image of me in the bathtub. Skin a pale pink like when I was first born. I am her only child. Now she'll get me anything.
"Tea dear?"
"Another slice of cake? Let me get that for you."
I look away when she stands up, now she needs a table or anything around her for support. Her arthritis is only getting worse.

5. ONE TIME SHE ASKED ME WHY.

And I honestly didn't know.

6. EVERY SUNDAY.

I would put on my best shoes and we would go to church together. One sermon stuck out the most. It was about Lucifer and his fallen angels and how they choose the bad side. And I've always wondered why.

7. FALLING.

After I awoke from a dreamless night in the hospital. I walked to the balcony in my room. I didn't understand the point of it being there if it was going to have a large heavy duty lock on its sliding door. If you recollect a dream its supposed to mean something. I don't know why, at that moment, I recalled a dream that took place so long ago. But I did. Looking out past the commercial greenery and black fencing, I realized that I am a fallen angel.

8. I MET AN ANGEL ONCE.

In high school. Her name was Alma. People at school called her a loser because she was missing a finger on her left hand. I couldn't fathom why people could be so cruel to such a pretty girl. I talked to her and she became one of my best friends. And then she left, and every night while I lay awake, I question what it is I said wrong to make her go away.

9. THE FINGER SHE LOST WAS THE RING FINGER.

We were both lying on her bed. Music was playing softly. A band she knew and that I grew to also like. Then suddenly she said: "It was a car accident. Many things were broken but my finger was unfixable. When I woke up and saw that they had removed it, I was furious to tears." I was silent. "From then on," she said, "I hated doctors. It's their job to fix things the human heart can't and they failed. Now no one will marry me." "I'll marry you," I said, and I meant it. She did not respond, instead she just waved her left hand in my face. I took it and held on to it, kissing the gap between the pinky and middle finger.

10. NINE IS AN UNLUCKY NUMBER.

It was the ninth month on the ninth day when she left. I remember it so vividly I could paint it. Except I'm no painter. I didn't have to see her face. I know I didn't.

But all I can remember is feeling this wave, of something, leave me. And maybe the canvas can contain such emotion but people might mistake it for a day at the beach, deep blues turning to black. I hated her but even though nine is a bad luck number, I loved every one of her fingers.

11.

Nights later, I had a dream that I was falling. After I woke up, I realized Alma wouldn't come back to me, that she couldn't. That I had to go to her, even if it meant giving up my slot in heaven just to hold her hand in hell.

12. TRY AGAIN.

Khat Patrong, Grade 11
Duke Ellington School of the Arts
Washington, DC
Flash Fiction, Gold Key and American Voices Nominee

the last stop
(excerpted)

The sun always looked forward to rising here. She liked bathing the dusty plain in blistering shades of red and gold and tossing the furious auburn waves behind her in a tremendous, blazing mantle, and when she stretched herself as far as she could, she could see the long horizon bloody with the new dawn. There was nothing to distract.

The only building for miles was hardly a diversion. Leaning sideways against the prairie gorse and bent double against the prairie wind was a simple single-floor wooden structure. The wood was clean but cracked with age, and there was a platform with posts for the roof that ran aside a bunch of old iron rails. In one direction the tracks beat strong into the sun, casting long shadows against the sky. They hammered the ground as if by clout or impetus they might impose prerogative on man and beast and brush; this path must be. In the other direction, the tracks ran only a little ways before stopping at a sign with letters painstakingly drawn in red paint: THE END. The last stop.

The stationmaster woke up and stretched. He gently slid out from underneath a large, greyish furry bundle sprawled across his chest. He made his bed and carefully folded it up. He smiled at the dandelion and pulled on his blue freshly ironed uniform and his cap with the gold braid and walked into the other room. This room had a desk and a chair in one corner and a tiny kitchen unit in another and a small dining table in between and all around there were comfortable squashy armchairs for the passengers to wait in and there was a big pile of packages, all different shapes and sizes stacked carefully in a third corner. The desk was very neat and organized, and the pencils were all in a mug, no delinquent rolling round on the smooth oaken surface, no stiff wooden body lying casualty on the floor. The stationmaster walked over to the door and yanked it open and yawned a good morning at the new day and walked back to the refrigerator and took out some eggs to make eggs Benedict (which the stationmaster never particularly enjoyed, but always felt it was something people had for breakfast and enjoyed and why not).

Over in the other room, the bundle was unraveling itself and stretching long, like water moving 'cross the hardwood floor, grace and awkward movements that were lovely in their animal sincerity. The stationmaster called him Gus. Gus was an Irish wolfhound, and those great consuls and glorious emperors were not remiss when they wrote of that fantastic species "all Rome viewed with wonder". Gus had a shaggy handsome face and a clumsy splendor that suited him perfectly.

The stationmaster carefully put the eggs on a plate and opened the cabinet to take down a teacup. There were two, which always made the stationmaster a little sad. He got out a saucer and poured some water for Gus and took out another saucer and put some of the lamb from last night into it with some rice and things, and then he poured some tea for himself and the two friends sat there eating sleepily as the shy dawn light crept in. They painted a handsome picture over breakfast, Gus with his large intelligent eyes and his beautiful grey-blue fur, and the stationmaster with his short greying curls and his wonderful grandfatherly mustache – the kind a granddaughter should like to pull softly for another story. But the stationmaster had no grandchildren.

It was time for work and he looked to Gus who stood and stretched and whuffled in the stationmaster's sleeve to say yes I'm ready too.

Being the stationmaster was a very exciting job. Incredibly interesting people came through and the stationmaster would ring for a train and while they were waiting he got to listen to incredibly interesting stories, so that he often felt he had traveled the world over. But it was very rare to get passengers and they always left on a train and he would watch until even the dust was gone and settled back into the ground and on his cap and his uniform and Gus's ears twitched with it and he stood very still so the dust was there for a long time and then he would turn and walk slowly back into the station.

More often, his job was (as the executive put it) to "catch the things that had gone on" and "send them home." He had found teddy bears and love letters and photos and keys and, once, a tooth. Sometimes, very, very important packages would come along, and he'd pick them up and set them aside – a treaty or a piece of evidence – and important people would come out and shake his hand and pat his back and talk about medals and stuff and then they'd be gone. And sometimes the same things would just keep coming back, and this made him sad because he knew this meant they had no home. So he did his best to make a home for them. Gus had been a lost thing.

Most often his job was just to keep the station in order. Together, he and Gus kept it ship-shape. They polished wood and restuffed chairs and dusted tracks (which was a battle let me tell you, with all the sand in that place) and repainted signs.

Today, they did all this and still had time before lunch. So the stationmaster scratched his head and Gus pawed his ears and then the stationmaster snapped his fingers and said they would fix the old clock. And so they took it down and opened it and fiddled with it a little and Gus had fun with the gears and the stationmaster got out his screwdriver and then it was fixed and time for lunch.

The stationmaster got them each a cucumber sandwich and they sat side by side on the little platform, and the stationmaster leaned against a post and Gus leaned against the stationmaster and they ate and watched the breeze work against the tall grass and though they made short work of the sandwiches, they did not move.

The stationmaster was thinking about the second teacup. He knew that his curls were turning grey and he could trace every year in the worry lines and the laugh crinkles that framed his eyes and carved over his forehead, but he was a strong man. He knew that he had lots of time left, and it was this exactly that frightened him. There would be exciting days, yes, but more often there would be this sort of day, and then there was only the station, and the tracks, and the wind that blew hard and fast and cut deep to an ache in his heart that he could not will away and that ache festered and burned so that he caught his breath in his throat. He blew out and tipped his cap forward a little so Gus would not see him cry.

Anna Pomper, Grade 11
Maret School
Washington, DC
Short Story, Gold Key

reflection

"Home is where the heart is."
Home is where there's a little sienna
    rug-or-mat-type-thing out front.
      Forget to clean your shoes off before you step in.
Home has a storm door.
Home has these big mahogany-colored wooden walls
    to keep out and keep well.

"Honey, I'm…"

Home is where you pushed a broken paper
    clip into your pale wrist
Home is where you tried not to stain
    your crisp sheets, your empty shelves,
    your fresh shoes with your
    dripping fingers, dripping eyes, dripping sarcasm –
Watch out or you'll slip
    Watch the TV, Watch the clock
    Look at my face when I speak to you,
      Your Full Name For Dramatic Effect –
Watch it unfold like clean shirts and linens
    in your body-odored closet
    Dripping out of place;
      Droplets in your sink that *Honey*
        never got around to.

A heart-shaped box half-filled with burnt
marshmallows and deck splinters.

But *Home* is also where you just rest your
    tired eyes – insist they're still trained on the monitor.

And *Home* is where you pretend to be asleep
    when they get home because I-and-you-and-they
    don't know why.
And it's a fine thing, to not know at *Home*.
    To sleep earlier than you would
        At *Home*

    That aging, oaken door you've slammed and locked;
    Those blinds you've shut because you just
        won't open those eyes to that sun;
    Those hand-me-down, beige brown khakis from
        an unknown brother that are so wide
        you've felt your flesh freely rippling
        and shaking inside them;

Take your hands off of your face.
Pay no attention to your mirror.
Stare at your heart's hard work 'til it sets into your
    fading porcelain.
Forever tarnish your tub with your muddy,
    coagulated memory –
        "When bombs drop, you know that's the
            best place to be."

Dario Sanchez. Grade 12
Sidwell Friends School
Washington, DC
Poetry, Silver Key

sharaf

Sharaf.
The sound of two languages
Combining, mixing in with
The soft scratching of a record
Finished but not removed
From the record player.

Sharaf.
A household
Filled with women
Leaving one man
To defend for himself.
Saffron and Dill,
Mint and Turmeric,
Blending in the air
Into a beautiful sensation.

But
Sharaf does not exist.
Sharaf is a fake disguise
To help the naïve become
More ignorant.
To aid those in their
Judgmental ways

Sharahshahi does exist.
An Iranian family
With roots back
Hundreds of thousands of years.
Sharafshahi is
The thick heat of

An extra layer of
Dark curly hair covering
Our bodies,
Along with a history.
Covering our identities
Which have changed over the years,
Though the change isn't seen.
Others eyes masked by the
Goggles of judgment
Placed on by the elders
Of judgments past.

Mona Sharaf, Grade 10
Duke Ellington School of the Arts
Washington, DC
Poetry, Honorable Mention

whispers of the past
(excerpted)

One day, when I was about five years old, the cleaning lady came at precisely nine o'clock in the morning to the house in New Delhi, India. I thought that she was there for just another normal day of sweeping and vacuuming the house, just as she did almost every other day of the week. However, something was unusual. There was a small boy peeking about timidly from behind the maid's back at the polished marble floor, the high arched ceiling, and the spiraling staircase that led to the upper floors of the house. I was curious and went to investigate. When I asked her who the boy was, the maid sorrowfully told me that it was her son, and that because his father had just passed away due to some mysterious disease (when I was older, I was able to infer that it was lung cancer, and that because the maid had no medical knowledge, nor, unfortunately, access to a doctor, she was unaware of such) after working in a factory, her son could not go to work with him to learn hard labor but had to start working soon in some way to make money for the family.

When I asked my mother about the new boy, she said that he and his mother came from a slum about five minutes away; our community was a beacon of hope that they came to in order to make a living. It was the base of their existence, and yet, after a hard day's work in a large house that they probably dreamed of living in, they had to return to the slums, with despair, hunger, and poverty awaiting them.

From that day on, his mother used to bring the boy about four times a week as she came to clean the house. Initially, he used to remain very silent and sat in a corner of the living room, never interacting with me. He appeared demoralized, as if life, though it had barely started, had already defeated him. We exchanged our first words no less than a full month after first meeting each other. I still remember that conversation.

"What are you writing?" a thin, shaky voice behind me asked. By now, I had gotten so used to him sitting quietly on the floor in a corner of the room that I had forgotten he was even present. It must have been a weekend day, as I was sitting in my living room, not a classroom, the ten o'clock morning rays filtering through the windows, bright, but not yet hot like they would become by noon. I looked at the paper I was writing on, the letters of the alphabet scrawled all over it, each one slightly disproportionate, as if it had been written with the hands of uncertainty.

"It's a homework assignment. I have to practice writing all the letters in under two minutes." He nodded in acknowledgement, and silence settled over the room once again, enveloping it much like a blanket would. Soon, I wanted to renew conversation, and asked him, "Do you know how to read and write the letters?"

He remained mute for several seconds, and finally, turned towards me slowly, shame evident in his eyes.

"No. I don't have enough money to go to school. And now that my father is dead, the little hope I had is also gone." I had never before pondered what life must be like for the destitute, even though, in India, with all of its new development, poverty was still very much evident.

Several days later, I found myself back in the same

position; it was another day, and the maid's son was in the corner again, as usual. This time, I addressed him.

"What's your name?"

He replied, "Veer."

"How old are you?"

"Five," came the shy answer.

"Oh! We're the same age! Would you like to learn how to read and write English, Veer?"

His head whipped towards me, and his mouth hung open in disbelief. Slowly, a smile began to spread across his face, and it seemed that his eyes shone.

"Y-yes!" he stammered. "I would like that very much!"

"Come, then! Let's start from the beginning!" I exclaimed.

"This is A," I said to him. "You draw a mountain, then a line in between."

I gave him a pencil and sheet of paper, and helped him trace the letter A. After that, I let him do it, and in no time, he had three perfect A's drawn on the paper. I nodded, satisfied.

Just a short time later, I was teaching Veer how to form Z. He was a very fast learner. In fact, he picked everything up faster than I had in school, I realized slightly enviously.

"Yeah, yeah, you're good," I told him, "but you're not as fast as I was at learning the alphabet."

From then on, his speed and focus rose to an even higher degree, to the point where he seemed to be learning all the concepts I taught him on sight, and I realized that he was much sharper and more intelligent that I was.

That night, I asked my mom why Veer wasn't allowed in school, despite the fact that he was perhaps the most intelligent kid of my age that I knew. My mother responded, with a sigh, that it was all about the money. I was able to attend school because I had money, even though I was not as qualified as Veer. I learned a very harsh reality about the world at that moment. There were few things in the world that money couldn't buy. It bought me a life of relative luxury and comfort, but a lack of money left the intelligent Veer out in the cold, at the edge of survival and death.

The next day, I reviewed the alphabet with Veer, an exercise that proved to be nearly futile, since he wrote them all in slightly over a minute, a time that surpassed my current best from my school homework.

Amazed, I finally admitted to him, "You're very good at this. You wrote all of the letters faster than I can! Since, you've already mastered the alphabet, I will now teach you words."

"A for apple. B for bat..." Thus began our strong bond as best friends, pouring over words and letters almost every day. Pretty soon, the three days of the week on which Veer didn't come to the house felt empty, as if some large aspect of my life was missing.

On the days he did arrive, his mind was as quick as ever, and in about two weeks, he had memorized many of the basic words associated with the letters, from apple, bat, cat, and dog, to wall, xylophone, yo-yo, and zebra.

"I'll teach you more words now, since you know the most basic ones. I started instructing you about a month ago, and you've already almost caught up to my preschool class, which I've been attending for about three months!"

Veer giggled, modesty and pride visible on his face at the same time, balancing each other out, just as many other things I had recently begun to notice; light and dark, justice and injustice, addition and subtraction, and strife and joy were all things that complemented each other.

Chaitanya Singh, Grade 10
Winston Churchill High School / Writopia Lab
Potomac, MD
Personal Essay, Honorable Mention

magician of change
(excerpted)

1. I used to have a collection of thumb drives.

One was a pig, one I had colored myself, others had the names of organizations I knew nothing about. They were filled with homework assignments, pictures I thought I was great at editing, coloring pages, and anything else I wanted to print out. I had to take the thumb drive into my parents' office and print things off from my dad's computer. I didn't mind doing this, because it meant I got to have a desktop in my room and that I could stay up past bedtime on chat rooms.

One time, I was waiting for my vocabulary list to print off, and I picked a piece of paper up off the printer. It was addressed to Hawaii, which should have concerned me from the get go since the only people we knew there were my dad's son and ex-wife. It was addressed, though, to a Buddhist monastery. I picked it up off the printer, and under it was a picture of my brother. I read only the first paragraph of the letter, that *Lee R. Smith is being investigated as a missing person in the state of Hawaii* and that *you were the last people he was known to have been in contact with.* At the bottom of the page, I saw my father's slim signature and his phone number. I thought that he wasn't supposed to give his phone number to strangers.

2. The word lost

is so vague. I hate it. There are so many better things that provide context, explanation or just specific information:

-I don't know where I am
-I don't know where I'm going
-I don't understand
-This doesn't seem familiar
-I misplaced something or left it somewhere

3. Learning about my brother was like putting together pieces of a puzzle.

After the letter, I only had my memory and little pieces of conversation. My family was strange, they weren't like the people in books or movies, they didn't shut down and stop talking about him. But after the initial search, they stopped questioning where he was or when he would return; it was like he was still indefinitely away in Chicago, obtaining his PhD. My family still spoke about my brother but not about his being missing. No one ever came out and told me that he was missing, maybe because children have no filters so someone might have asked: Is he dead? No one ever said, "Lee isn't coming home tonight." He just didn't.

4. Was and is are the two most confusing tenses in the dictionary.

He was. He is.

5. I had this obsession with mental illness.

One night at dinner, I started on a spiel of 'Did You Know?':

"Did you know bipolar disorder was originally called manic depression? Yeah, 'cause people who are bipolar go through periods of mania and then of depression."

"Yes," my mother replied.

My father nodded.

"Lee has bipolar disorder," my mother said -- as if it was hers to share.

My dad was always a teacher to me, so he explained to me the things about bipolar disorder that I wouldn't have read online. Like, during the mania, people with bipolar disorder can be a lot of fun and that at times people will go off their meds to experience mania again, but it usually backfires when people start to feel depressed. The information sounded like more than a textbook response and I wondered who had put the implications there -- me or him -- because if it had been me, then I was certainly wrong but my father only lied about stupid stuff.

6. I am self-diagnosed with bipolar disorder.

Because I understand the reasoning, and I know I shouldn't.

7. My father lies about stupid stuff.

When I was little, he would make me memorize math problems, and if, after a week, I knew the answer, he would give me a dollar. They were simple things; the hardest one for me was eight times seven. He taught me how to remember things with rhythm: eight -- *snap* -- times -- *snap* -- sev -- *snap* -- en *snap* -- equals -- *snap* fif -- *snap* -- ty *snap* -- six. He said if I could learn that -- eight times seven equals fifty six -- I could learn anything. On Friday nights, before falling asleep to the sound of him reading, he would ask me the math problem, and if I got it right we would go into the top drawer of his dresser where he kept all the cool stuff. He would ask me if I wanted a dollar bill or a dollar coin, and I would always pick coins because they were prettier.

One day, I went to the school store to buy a scented pencil and a hedgehog-shaped eraser, and I handed the lady the coins I had earned. At first she laughed, then a look of understanding, she leaned in and very gently told me that my dollar coins were, in fact, poker chips.

8. My father is dyslexic.

Sometimes he spells 'Chesapeake' 'Chespeke' or he asks me how to spell 'anniversary' and I look at him like he is the stupidest man in the world. But really, I think my daddy is smarter than all my teachers and all the gurus. People talk about the moment they realize their fathers are simply men, but my daddy is the closest thing there is to God. In spite of it all, my father has the courage to sit down with me and help with my homework. Sometimes I wish it didn't take him ten minutes to write a sentence so that I could read his story.

9. My brother is lost.

10. At some point, they started calling his bedroom the guest bedroom.

I don't know when exactly it started, but it quickly became consistent. Once I noticed, it bothered me. I started saying *Lee's bedroom* with a purposeless sense of purpose. His paintings still hang on the walls, his graduation cap is still in the closet and the strange trinkets he brought from all over the world are in his nightstand.

Guest bedroom didn't really stick; it negated his whole existence as anything other than a guest in our lives and so, with a lack of any somberness, we started to call it simply The Bedroom.

Barrett Smith, Grade 11
Duke Ellington School of the Arts
Washington, DC
Personal Essay, Gold Key

the housekeeper's daughter

Porsches, pools, Pomeranians, Prada, and Polo are all essentials of the upper class. These folks are fortunate to arrive to a nice clean home every night with the floors vacuumed, the beds made, and the toilets scrubbed. This cleanliness is not an act of magic, but simply a mission completed by a middle-aged Colombian woman and her American-born daughter.

Take Your Daughter to Work Day was never a big hit with me. My mother is a housekeeper and Take Your Daughter to Work Day happens to be on school holidays and summer vacations. Growing up, I used to be ashamed of her job. The other kids had doctors, accountants, and lawyers as parents. I used to make up lies when my friends would ask me what my mother did for a living. I would say she had her own business, which is for the most part true. But after a while I realized that my mother worked harder than all those parents combined. She comes home dead tired from cleaning houses and still manages to drive me to practice and make fantastic lasagna for dinner. She is the hardest worker I know and for that I now proudly declare that my mother is a housekeeper. When I go to work with her, I am there to work. She has bestowed onto me her strong work ethic and dedication. It does not matter whether the Johnsons never use their guest bathroom; the bathroom better have the best looking mirrors in the world.

The Ten Commandments of Going to Work with My Mother
1. Dress presentably
2. Greet the bosses with Sir or Ma'am
3. Don't eat their food
4. Don't steal ANYTHING
5. Don't break ANYTHING
6. Be quiet
7. Don't speak Spanish (When you do the bosses think you're talking about them)
8. Don't be in a bad mood
9. Always help when needed
10. Never be jealous of what they have

Dish Washer

Washing plates and cups is my most dreaded assignment. It's not that I'm not good at it, because, truthfully, I was born to wash plates and cups. It's not that I'm completely against washing plates; it's simply that I don't like washing other people's plates. Yes, I do clean other people's houses, but I draw the line at plates, cups, and silverware. It makes me feel as if I am a servant and they are lazy royals who can't simply wash their own tableware.

Dusting

"My oh my, Maria, that little girl of yours puts so much carefulness into dusting!" the employers of my mother would say to her, as they would watch me dust and re-dust an office desk ten times. To them, I was particular to details, but to me, I was a spy snooping for information. When they weren't looking I would simply skim at already opened letters. Of course my mother would scowl at me when she saw me snooping and tell me to do my job and mind my own business. Dusting gave me chances to look at photo albums, yearbooks, magazines, agendas, and holiday cards. My favorites were the holiday cards, especially the ones where the families wore matching sweaters. Snooping not only contributed to my personal entertainment, but it allowed me to match my story to the employer.

Windex

When you're the housekeeper's daughter, you have a favorite assignment. My favorite assignment is using Windex. It is a magical substance which you can use for practically anything. Probably one of my biggest pet peeves is a dirty mirror, but Windex can turn that dirty mirror into a crystal clear portal.

Sponge

Although I do use a sponge when I clean, I also act like a sponge as I listen. Most wealthy people are interesting and live exciting lives. They have funny occurrences, which they tell their sisters. They have complaints about their spouses, which they tell their mother. My favorite conversations are the political discussions. Even though I do not consider myself politically informed, discussions about politics are simply fascinating. I always get excited when I drive towards an employer's home and see a political sign. Folks are very passionate about their politics. They defend their views as if they were their own children.

The Family

The Sir and Ma'am of the household are usually kind. They always greet you and ask how school is. When you're little they are sometimes nice enough to set up the TV for you and offer you a snack, which you have to decline. Some send fruit baskets or toys for

Christmas. If they have children, you are usually friends with them and often watch movies or swim in their pool. If they have grown up children, you normally get their hand-me-downs, which isn't half bad when the brands range from Coach, Juicy Couture, and Victoria's Secret to Polo.

Confessions

It irritates me when families monitor their home as we clean as if they are not able to trust my five foot two mother. I hate it when they stare at me as I clean. They are simply setting me up to break a priceless heirloom. However, the absolute worst thing is to hear that my mother is fired from a job. It happens and I understand that having a housekeeper is a luxury and in tough times people tighten their budgets. I'm a reasonable person, but seeing your mother sad about losing a job is always rough.

Gratefulness

Employers can be cranky and picky, but they provide for my family and I appreciate them for that. Doing manual labor has also instilled a strong desire for me to succeed. Seeing all the luxuries people are able to afford does make me jealous, but it makes me jealous enough to want to work hard in school and get a well-paying job. Of course I would rather have my mother be a secretary and not have to work so hard, but because of her job she was able to take me to work on school holidays and not have to pay for a sitter. She is also able to pick her own hours and is always there in the morning before I go to school and there in the afternoon when I get back. It is always difficult to get up early in the summer and clean, but my mother cleans eight days a week and doesn't complain. My mother makes so many sacrifices for my family. I really do appreciate her dedication, patience, commitment and perseverance.

I am the Housekeeper's daughter and I am **proud** of my mother.

Carolina Sosa, Grade 10
Westfield High School
Chantilly, VA
Personal Essay, Silver Key

a self portrait

I'm 17.
And as the day drags on I've yet to grow into my
shadow
and though parts of me yearn to be mistaken for the
sun dial, I'm still always latest to the party.
I'm a Sagittarius.
I was born on the cusp of winter.
My mother was born in September, and sometimes I
fear I was the first snow of her youth.
When I lie in bed some nights, I mistake my heartbeat
for a ticking clock.
I bring things to my nose to see how they will feel
nocked in my cupid's bow.
I touch them to make sure my fingerprints leave a
mark.
I didn't learn to tie my shoes properly 'til I was 15-and-
a-half.
I'm fluent in Russian, but I refuse to memorize the
order of the alphabet.
The great-grandmother I was named for gathered her
life with half-an-hour's pin point precision and sent her
son on a train to where the air was cold enough to
freeze war in its tracks.
My grandfather wore hope in the shape of a knitted hat
on the day of his second birth.
His sister saved his life.
Every day I wade knee-deep in my improbability.
When my father's mother twiddles her thumbs, I see
my reflection.
When I was four, I mistook pictures of his child's face

for mine.
I am bursting to give these things away
to be discovered.
Hold me up to the light like a dollop of amber.
Watch silver tulle ghost tails slither through my veins.
You can use them for a transfusion if you like;
let's pray we have the same blood type.

Polina Tamerina, Grade 12
McLean High School
McLean, VA
Poetry, Silver Key

raw feet

oddly numb behind my aspirations tonight
oddly terrified of the upcoming weeks
of christmas time and lights and these things that used
to be so sweet
greatly involved in my own mind
in my heart I can see your smile
and in my bones I can feel the way
our raw feet used to slap the cold concrete
on grandmother's front porch
imagining they were all
out to get us
and now we don't have to pretend
now we choose not to hide
but only indulge ourselves in this place
much similar to a beehive.
(say it like this: bee h-ive)
and I can taste in my mouth the tart reminder
of loss and what else can I say
of it
my legs covered in black cloth and my chest soaked in
an ocean blue,
everything only lasts for a moment
the moment is present and soon far away
but my existence is a gathering of these segments
mixed up and bound by yarn, clothes-pins, and
photographs
with rounded edges
my reflection becomes unreal, forming a two
dimensional excuse
to move and watch the shadows change the pigment of
my face

and I feel my bones again,
raw feet slapping the cold concrete.

Elisabeth Tropea, Grade 12
Centreville High School
Clifton, VA
Poetry, Silver Key

detaching from stigmas

There are over 800,000 youth served in the foster care system each year in the United States. July 25th, 2010, was the day I became a part of that statistic.

As a ward of the state, I endured many obstacles and watched as my peers moved forward without the skills to pursue their goals in life. Inspired by youth who feel defeated, and the struggles I have faced in foster care, my hunger to strive for success grew dramatically. Chasing my dream of becoming an artist inspired me to change my life and make a difference in the lives of others.

Statistically, I am incapable of success. But I have detached myself from stigmas and made my own path. Mental faith, my art, and intrinsic motivation are what will close a chapter in my life and begin the writing of a new one.

In my eyes, my childhood was like any other. My mother had dreams of creating a perfect family foundation for my brother and me. She never had ideal circumstances in her family when she grew up, and so she tried to give us the life she always wanted as a child. My mother lived up to her expectations and pushed me in school to do my best. However, raising two children as a single mother in madness was a challenge.

We lived in the projects where gunshots every night were the norm and the deaths of youth were a part of life. Even though my mother had placed me in a good school, coming home was a reality for me. The environment around me began to mold my mind like clay, forming a negative perception on life. The words my mother had told me – that I could become whatever

I wanted – began to evaporate and so did my dreams, ascending in midair.

Freshman year of high school was a manifestation of my misconceptions. I took more pride in hanging outside of the classroom than getting an education inside the classroom. Peer pressure dictated my decisions and steered me through a path of failure and the lack of belief I had in myself. It seemed the only thing that I put my full attention into was drawing. But my grades plummeted, and this prevented me from taking an advanced art class.

So I tried an Art One class. I was relieved that I had the opportunity to express myself and actually wanted to be engaged in a classroom setting. Unfortunately, everyone has to have art credits, which means I had to be in a classroom of peers that didn't appreciate art. A couple of days into the class, a paint fight broke out and, as a consequence, we were banned from using the materials. We had to do book work for the rest of the term.

The one thing that motivated me was now not what I had envisioned. Ultimately, I just gave up and continued to become society's negative expectations of a black kid who grew up in the ghetto. I couldn't hide bad grades and my lack of applying myself in school from my mother any longer. She was disappointed in me, but mostly blamed herself as a parent. I had failed my ninth grade year and had to repeat it. The kid that sat at the window and watched the destruction of her community, who had vowed to never become a part of the madness, was now just a little girl making promises to herself.

I wanted to find my way back to my morals and what I believed in. I didn't know how or what I had to do, but I was ready for a change and a new start on my education. I had gained the confidence, but I didn't anticipate the obstacles that were yet to come.

I was oblivious to how close my mother was to her breaking point. I had never thought she would abuse substances to cope with the obstacles life had put in front of her. But she gave up on life and me.

It was the first semester of school and I had a lot on my mind. During this time my school was out of bounds from where I lived and the commute was long. My mother became so consumed with substances she stopped going to work and did not help me get back and forth to school. I couldn't recognize the person she had become; she no longer took on the role of a parent, but of an addict.

I couldn't comprehend the gravity of my situation and the impact it had on my education. I started showing up later and later to school, and then I started to miss day after day. The school kept track of my attendance and tried reaching out to my mother, but she was too wrapped up in her depression, like a wingless fly trapped in the web of a black widow. I figured that if my mother didn't care about my education, then why should I?

With an absent mother and an older brother incarcerated, there was no one to take care of me. I was placed in the Foster Care system.

This obstacle was something that I would have to overcome if I didn't want to join the ranks of my loved ones. But I made a choice. I chose life. It had not dawned on me during the first two weeks of being in someone else's home that it would turn into two and a half years before I would reunite with my mother.

Things were not the way I was told they would be in my new foster home. I started to realize that my foster parent had taken me in to make ends meet, not because my best interest was at heart. I felt as though I was being thrown into another world, something more foreign than what I was used to. I was struggling with both the lack of parenting and becoming accustomed to strangers. When I would reach out for help from people within the Child and Family Service Agency (CFSA) for answers, it was like moving a mountain. I was getting nowhere; no one cared and no one listened.

That is when it all hit me like a ton of bricks: I was on my own. I knew that I had to fight with everything I had and I knew it was not going to be easy.

I was attending a new school, Luke C. Moore Academy. This was my first year attending a DC public school since I was 6 years old. It was a brand new environment to adjust to. I did not have a post-high school plan. Ultimately, I wanted out of everything. The only solution I could think of was to run so I wouldn't have to deal with all my problems.

I geared towards going to Job Corps, because that was my ticket out of CFSA. I just did not want to have to live with strangers that did not care about my well-being or me. And then I was removed from my foster home and into a new foster home placement.

I was an emotional wreck. The grief over my mother's absence was the same as the pain over a loved one's death. Stress and depression was my next big hurdle. I can vaguely remember times that I would attend school after sleeping only one or two hours. There was a time when I could not get out of the bed for three days straight, because I missed my mother and I was unable to see her. But I knew that if I let my circumstances get the best of me, I would not make it. It was up to me to pull the pieces together because if I did not, no one else would.

Things began to progress and I started to express my feelings through my drawings more. I was finally enrolled in an Art One class and I made a connection with the art teacher. At first, I was not receptive to her advice or her opinions. We fought until the end. After I passed and was no longer in her classes, I realized that she had done what no one else had – that is, encourage me, even when I felt I was incapable. She raised my awareness of the endless possibilities I could achieve with my art. She opened my eyes to a world I have never seen before and I knew that this was it.

I had lived, breathed, and created art my whole life. So when my art teacher showed me art schools, I became consciously aware that I had a passion for art and that I wanted to pursue it. I knew she was the person to help guide me on achieving my goal of being an artist. We were a team and the minute she knew of opportunities for me to showcase my talent, she brought it to my attention.

School was finally going the way I wanted. I applied myself and challenged myself, even while going through the perils of CFSA and coping with my family's circumstances. My commute was an hour and a half, back and forth to school every day. Instead of complaining I used my commute to my benefit and read books to better myself. I stayed after school and demanded extra work.

My art teacher believed in me when no one else did. That was very important to me. Because I was unable to receive encouragement from my mother or foster parent and around this time, I was lost without any guidance in my life. Ultimately, I began to recognize the potential everyone was seeing in me. I was blossoming into a rare flower in a garden of invasive species. I became aware of my surroundings and the world around me. I discovered who I was and the impact I could have on others. I was not only going to tell my story through my art, I was going to make a change.

Khadija Wilson, Grade 12
Luke C. Moore Academy Senior High School
Washington, DC
Personal Essay, Gold Key

artist's haiku

my brush dabbles in
the black paint, and rings form round
the puddle of black

black strokes on the page;
dark clouds fill the water bowl
at my brush's touch

*

a click punctuates
the silence, as my fingers
press on the keyboard

the thin, blinking line
appears, marking where my words
have stopped clicking out

i lean back slowly,
let my eyes spill across the
black, spindly letters

*

the creamy white keys
are begging me to press them;
i do so gently

i hear the hollow
echoing, whispering in
the huge piano

again, i press down,
harder, this time, so the notes
are serenading

more, more, more, i think,
and my fingers flood the keys
a dancing river

*

i grip and squeeze hard;
the thick oil paint slithers out
creamy and gaudy

smears of bright, bright paint
squeezed, dented tubes, littering
the fold-up table

grip the brush handle
gleaming reddish wood that shines
under my lamp's light

the fine hairs sprawl out
as the brush touches the page
dabbing on color

Julia Winkler, Grade 7
Little Flower School
Bethesda, MD
Poetry, Gold Key

on loving a sad boy

1
You tell me a story about the monster inside of you,
how it is ferocious and large and full of
Nothingness.
It gobbles down bunnies and flowers and the hearts
of people like me,
but I know this tale already.

2
Some days, being with you
is like being asleep when the actual Peter Pan drops by
because I am always missing out
on the chance to fly.

3
I miss you all the time.
Even when you are here
it is only your shadow
which you have lost a hold of
once again.

4
You ask me what it's like
to love an incomplete person.
I tell you my story:
your body is one land and mine another
but I am learning to fence and grapple and sail
across a galaxy.

5
You are the only
lost boy
I want.

6
I press myself into your neck and linger to
count the spaces between heartbeats,
one silence after another.
I never understand the words you are shouting
with each silence you bring but
my body is the plank on Captain Hook's ship
and every step you take can be careful and fragile
as long as you
stay here
and do not jump.

Megan Yan, Grade 12
Richard Montgomery High School
Rockville, MD
Poetry, Silver Key

rebirth revenge

There's something sly about the atmosphere,
the smirking crack of dead leaves at my feet,
sun dripping like hot wax down,
down
the back of my neck.

The sound barriers on highways let all sorts
of noises through,
and blink their graffiti eyes with an
insolent languor.
The spiders I crush and flush away
crumple their legs before the towel hits them,
brown, crooked omens.

The water in the sink scorches my hands,
the air shimmers with the
wavering cackle
of airborne gasoline.

Paper cuts refuse to close, the wind is too soft.
Everywhere things laugh at me.
The trees that used to breathe for my benefit wheeze
out
whispers of Mercutio's curse,
point the frayed tips of their tar-blackened branches.

"You," they say.
Heartbeats.
Ebbing thrusts of slow-sap veins.
"You will die too."

I can't decompose and grow again my soul.
I can't hold the gaze of the moon
where the man in black sits,
melting pleasure on a spoon.

The sulfurous air burns my eyes
and drinks,
long, slow swallows of
the saran-wrap tears that scald my face.
The sulfurous air laughs
gusts of yellow
through the cigarette parks where
dreamers
go to realize that
all things end.
God's things,
good things,
dead things
all have their marvelous end.

Emily Yaremchuk, Grade 12
Oakton High School
Vienna, VA
Poetry, Gold Key

afterword

We were both once teenagers who wrote.

We wrote in our journals about people we loved and lost, about fights with our moms, fights with our friends, about a confusing new world of dating and eating disorders and drinking, about good days at school, bad days at school, about our confusion over wanting boyfriends and then not wanting them. We wrote, with intensity, about everything.

It was not an option not to pick up the pen. Our whole hearts – sometimes broken – could be found in those high school notebooks. We spilled every messy emotion, every confession onto the page. We remember what it felt like to live every day so vividly, with such consequence.

But now, looking back, we understand that something has changed. We're not as raw as we used to be.

There are benefits to this, of course, but we also miss it. As adults, we're expected to mask strong emotion, tone it down, deal with it. But dangerous honesty is the lifeblood of good writing. And as adult writers, we often have to peel back that mask in order to get to that open place. We're more aware of the risks involved in baring it all, and of the courage it takes to put ourselves on the page.

The teens in this collection don't wear masks. Their vulnerability is front and center, on full display. Science tells us that adolescent brains are wired for taking risks, for exploring the unknown, and as scary as that may sound to a parent, to a reader, that is poignant and compelling and bold. We're thinking in particular about the teens who shared personal and sometimes painful stories within this collection. That takes guts. That takes confidence and purpose and a true generosity of heart. When we share these private truths, they become public connection. When we explore together these depths, we understand that we are not alone.

We feel honored and fortunate to work with teenagers on their writing because we have the opportunity to relive this intensity, to witness this bravery. We see it in our Writopia Lab workshops, in the submissions we read for the Scholastic Awards, and now, in the works celebrated in this anthology. These teen writers inspire us to face the blank page again ourselves, knowing that it's OK to be messy and unsure, as long as we are being real.

The teenage years are a raw, beautifully intense and passionate time. Maybe during these years we know the whole course of our lives are changing, because we're growing up. We know it's not going to last to be a teenager – the consuming changes, the first-blush discoveries – so we've got to capture it, hold it still. That is our charge to you, teen readers and writers. Live fully in this moment. Put the words on the page.

Kathy Crutcher
DC Director
Writopia Lab

Elizabeth Gutting
DC Program Manager
Writopia Lab

acknowledgments

The authors of the works published in this book recognize with gratitude all those who have helped us make this happen. We are honored by the awards we have received and are grateful to Writopia Lab for administering The Scholastic Writing Awards in Greater Washington.

We would like to thank Busboys and Poets for being the headline sponsor of the program. They have been a tremendous community partner on many fronts, including hosting our events and creating the Busboys and Poets Scholarship for the top senior portfolio in the region. We're glad to have such a cool literary and cultural force in the area supporting us.

We also thank Politics and Prose for their sponsorship and their hosting of a reading for Greater Washington's national medal winners. The Hill Center in Capitol Hill is also a sponsor, and they hosted free Scholastic Awards workshops and this year's judging day. The Maret School generously provided its library for our use during this publishing process.

Many other organizations and individuals contributed to the running of The Awards in DC. The DC Area Writing Project serves as a partner organization to Writopia Lab and was integral to the recruitment of jurors. More than forty different professional writers and editors served as jurors, carefully evaluating over 1000 submissions of poetry, scripts, and prose. The following local writers also served as proofreaders for this book: Steve Feldstein, Nicole Lee Idar, Taehee Kim, Alison Klein, Tony

Mancus, and Cristin Terrill. We are grateful for the time, energy, and resources offered by all.

We chose the cover art from among the hundreds of recognized pieces in this year's Scholastic Art Awards in the Greater Washington area. This image, entitled "Lava Rust" is digital photography by Sara Meyer of Edison High School. Thanks to Bradley Gutting for finalizing the cover design.

We give thanks to Kathy Crutcher and Elizabeth Gutting at Writopia Lab for organizing the creation of this book and for spreading awareness throughout Greater Washington of the opportunities that The Scholastic Writing Awards provides. We thank the Alliance for Young Artists & Writers for running the program across the country and for making all of this possible.

Finally, we are grateful for the teachers, family, and friends who helped guide us to write and submit these award-winning works, and for young artists everywhere, who walk the world with raw feet and live to tell about it.

recognition of teachers

The following teachers served as mentors and/or Awards sponsors for the authors of this book. We are grateful for their support, guidance, and encouragement.

John Adams, Jenni Ashley, Martha Beall, Judith Bello, Brian Borah, Richard Carlson, Michelle Cobb, Sarah Congable, Kathy Crutcher, Michael Dickel, Michelle Edwards, Lisa Friedman, Catherine Frum, Michael Greiner, Nancy Hannans, Robert Helmer, Danielle Hicks, Katherine Hovanec, Tracey Hughes, Katrina Jax, Sinta Jimenez, Kelly Knarr, Marni Leikin, Rosanna Marsh, Koye Oyedeji, Shelby Pastora, Matthew Quinn, Libbie Roberts, Diana Rye, Kendall Schuller, Jennifer Seavey, Davina Smith, John Stewart, Susan Sullivan, Kelli Taylor, Lori Wagoner, Lissa Waldman, Christine Wiedemann, and Jill Zupancic

about the book's creators

The following writers gathered together on February 10, 2013 at the Maret School in Washington, DC to design, edit, copyedit, and market this book.

Luisa Banchoff , 17 – When I'm not writing, I'm reading, analyzing, singing, or simply coming up with another idea.

Sarah Cooke, 17 – I am a desperate believer in things that are not real.

Barrett Smith, 16 – You won't get to know me by reading this sentence so I won't bother writing it.

Rachel Page, 14 – I write because it's easier than speaking out loud.

Caroline Ewing , 17 – I do not have much to say, but there is much I have to whisper.

Genevieve Kules, 17 – On a mission to save the world.

Kateri Gajadhar, 15 – Sometimes I manage to capture my elusive thoughts and corral them onto paper.

Elizabeth Lasater-Guttmann, 17 – Art is everywhere; it's just a matter of finding it.

Brittany Cheng, 17 – I am an aspiring writer and journalist, who enjoys playing guitar and lacrosse, and keeping up with my favorite DC sports teams.

Khat Patrong, 16 – I'm not the ordinary cat.

Katarina Holtzapple, 15 – I write in hopes that one day the adventures I come up with might happen to me.

Asia Alston, 16 – I refuse to be labeled as a poet or writer because I am much more than that, maybe much less.

Ben Koses, 18 – Sometimes my tongue is clumsy, but my pen is graceful and my thoughts are ink.

Mona Sharaf, 16 – I'm a strong believer in the power of music and Chunkey Monkey ice cream.

Gillian Page, 14 – I love good music and rainy afternoons.

Anwar Omeish, 16 – I'm an activist and a writer, a reader and a traveler, a dreamer and a scholar; passion is the crux of my existence.

Carolina Sosa, 15 – I'm currently making my cant's into cans and my dreams into plans.

Anasuya Lyons, 12 – I refuse to believe that magic is not real, as many people have told me, because I can see it all around me in what I read and write, and breathe.

Alessandra Lowy, 14 – When I'm not pouring my emotions onto paper, I enjoy expressing them musically or capturing beautiful moments of life through the snap of a camera.

Mari Baz, 18 – Some of the most beautiful words are discovered in pages of novels.

Lara Haft, 17 – This is the cast-iron sorting of magic and tangles. It is the Hudson and its cable bridge, the polemic, the birdsong.

Jen McLish, 14 – I write because it only rains ever so often and the world could use a drink.

Matthew Evenson, 12 – My words are butterflies that tickle the mind.

Mina Cooper, 13 – When I write, I can do anything in the world.

Rafael Lopez, 14 – I fanboy a lot.

Elisabeth Tropea, 17 – I write because I am in love with words and language, I read because of the identities they take on by the one who writes them.

Mimi Nguyen, 16 – I write what the world makes me live, experience, feel, and see. I write my truth.

Belen Edwards, 14 – If you guessed that I like writing, congrats, you're psychic!

Elena Asofsky, 13 – I am a realistic, logical Idealist who likes to make contradictory statements and look at the world through the kaleidoscope that is my own imagination.

Chaitanya Singh, 15 – I like to write about my own experiences, which help shape my perception of the world as a diverse place where hard work can help obtain almost anything.

about writopia lab

Writopia Lab is a 501(c)3 non-profit organization that hosts after-school, weekend, and summer creative writing workshops for writers ages 8-18. Through small, student-centered workshops led by published writers, Writopia Lab aims to help students become comfortable with expressing themselves on the page and to ultimately cultivate or maintain in them a love of writing. Writopia Lab serves as the Regional Affiliate for the Scholastic Writing Awards and administers the program throughout Greater Washington. Visit **www.writopialab.org** for more information, or contact Kathy Crutcher, DC Director, at kathy@writopialab.org.

about the scholastic writing awards

The Scholastic Art & Writing Awards is the largest, longest-running, most prestigious recognition program for creative teens in the country. In 2013, teens in grades 7-12 from public, private, and home schools throughout the U.S. and its territories submitted over 200,000 works of art and writing for a chance at recognition, publication, exhibition, and scholarships. Since 1923, The Awards have recognized more than 13 million students and made available over $25 million in scholarships. Visit **www.artandwriting.org** for more information.

Made in the USA
Middletown, DE
04 January 2018